presenting...

presenting...

Sister NoBlues

by hattie gossett

Firebrand
Books
Ithaca, New York

Selections from this book have appeared previously in *Conditions, Essence, Heresies, Jazz Spotlite News, Pleasure and Danger: Exploring Female Sexuality* (Routledge & Keegan Paul), *Southern Africa, Union-Wage,* and the *WREE Newsletter.*

Music Lyrics:

"Take Five" by Dave Bruback/Paul Desmond on *Take Five—Carmen McRae and Dave Bruback—Live at Basin Street East* (Columbia Records/CS 2316).

"Freight Train Blues" by Dorsey/Murphy on *Women's Railroad Blues* (Rosetta Records/RR 1301/1980, originally recorded on Paramount/1924).

"In The Red" by Lincoln/Bayen/Roach (Melotone Music/BMI) on *Straight Ahead* (Jazzman/ JAZ 5043/1981, originally recorded on Candid Records/8015/1961).

"Backlash Blues" by Nina Simone/Langston Hughes (Rolls Royce Music/ASCAP) on *Nina Simone In Concert* (Accord/SN 7108).

"I'm Gettin' 'Long Alright" by Bobby Sharpe/Charles Singleton (Marvin/ASCAP) on *Burnin'/ Live At Freddie Jet's Pied Piper, L.A.* (Atlantic Records/SD 1565/1970).

"Smooth Talk" on *Smooth Talk* (RCA/APL 1-2466).

"How I Got Over" by Clara Ward on *Mahalia Jackson's Greatest Hits* (Columbia Records/CS 8804).

"Wild Women Don't Have The Blues" by Ida Cox on *Wild Women Don't Have The Blues* (Rosetta Records/RR 1304/1981, originally recorded on Riverside Records/1961).

"Come Up And See Me Some Time" by Arthur Swanstrom/Louis Alter on *Ethel Waters' Greatest Hits* (Columbia Records, John Hammond Collection/KG 31571/1972, originally recorded on Brunswick Records/6885/March 30, 1934).

"Freedom Time" by Tillery/Watkins (Tuizer Music/ASCAP) on *Linda Tillery* (Olivia Records/ 1977).

"Womanly Way" by Tillery/Watkins/Lindsay (Tuizer Music/ASCAP) on *Linda Tillery* (Olivia Records/1977).

"Trying Times" by Donny Hathaway/Leroy Hutson (Don-Pow/BMI) on *First Take* (Atlantic Records/SD 8230/1969).

"Yes We Can Can" by Allen Toussaint (Warner/Tamerlane/BMI) on *The Pointer Sisters* (Blue Thumb Records).

"Straight Ahead" by Lincoln/Baker/Waldron (Melotone Music/BMI) on *Straight Ahead* (Jazzman/JAZ 5043/1981, originally recorded on Candid Records/8015/1961).

Book design by Mary A. Scott
Cover design by Wendy Kenigsberg
Typesetting by Bets Ltd.

Printed on acid-free paper in the United States by McNaughton and Gunn

Library of Congress Catalog Card Number: 88-30146
ISBN 0-932379-50-8 (alk. paper)
ISBN 0-932379-49-4 (pbk.: alk. paper)

acknowledgments

i didn't make a list of the names of the people whose support for this book demands acknowledgment cuz i was scared i might slip up and forget somebody and get myself in a big mess of trouble. however i will say that this first book of mine which includes material written between 1975&1988 comes to you as a live&direct result of the energies of many people.

in fact you wouldn't even be holding this book in your hands right now dear reader had it not been for the longtime friends   support group sisters   students&colleagues   the therapist   wimmin writers   new friends   various underground renegades   the literary agent   the tipster   & the publisher who at one time or another read&commented on the individual pieces as they were written   who read&commented on the manuscript as it passed through several incarnations. i mean the people who affirmed   assured   stroked   soothed   prayed for   put up with   needled   annoyed   laughed at   infuriated   fell out with   ignored   forgot about   cajoled   pushed   understood   encouraged   appreciated   reflected &reaffirmed me as i went through my changes with this book.

to all of them i am everlastingly grateful and can think of no better way of expressing my gratitude than by repeating these words from sly stone:

> *i wanna*
> *thank you*
> *for lettin me*
> *be myself*
> *again.*

contents

section #4: some final hits/coming through the cracks

born into this life the child of house niggahs and been strugglin
tryin to get home ever since

a few days after april 11 1942 i was carried from the hospital to the room that was my parents quarters up over the garage of the house that belonged to the white folks they were working for as a live in maid and chauffeur couple. mama and daddy had come up north to strive for the better things in life like many others like them cuz ww2 was in high gear and lots of folks were leaving southern cities and farms (again) looking for a brighter day that included a piece of the post-depression change that the war industry was generating. like others like them mama and daddy believed that hard work thrift honesty and unquestioning respect for authority would be recognized and rewarded. they busted their asses and worked their fingers to the bone and when their dreams were brutally deferred they didnt explode like langston hughes says in his poem. instead they imploded and pinned their hopes on their children determined that we would miraculously come to be guests at the table which they could only serve and polish.

mama and daddy tried their best to start me off the right way along strivers row. they tried everything they and others like them could think of. after they split up when i was around 3 or 4 and mama took me to live in the projects and she went

to work on the car factory assembly line and dad-
dy went to live in a furnished room and worked as
a chauffeur sometimes and sometimes at the same
car factory as mama they kept on trying telling me
i had to grow up to be a lady and a credit to the
race and all and telling me i was better than the
other kids in the projects and why couldnt i speak
in wellmodulated pearshaped tones and play nice
by myself with my toys.

having me ride to school with my daddy in the
white folks cadillac (him in his chauffeurs uniform
and me in my catholic school girls uniform) cuz
they were scared to let me walk the few blocks
through the streets to school.

let me tell you that a black girl who is precocious
and adventuresome and asks a lot of questions and
who is also sensitive and somewhat timid and cries
easily who grows up in the projects with parents
who are always telling her not to cuss or fight
(skills that are vitally necessary for survival in the
projects) and to be a lady and a good negro (skills
that will get you killed in the projects) has it hard.

especially if she is big for her age and so scared
to fight thanks to mamas threats to whip her good
if there was ever any talk about her fighting in the
streets or at school and daddy telling her to obey
mama that she becomes an easy mark for bullies
half her own considerable size.

believe me this young girl has it hard especially
if at an early age she is aware of the difference in
the line her mama is running and her daddy is
supporting and the reality of life in the projects.

by 5th grade i got tired of getting beat up all the
time and not defending myself. one day in the
playground when the bullies had me cornered i
decided to fight back and so surprised the bullies
and myself with my heretofore hidden fire that
they eased up offa me from then on.

the fire continued making itself felt. i was always
questioning things i was supposed to accept on
blind faith. this annoyed my parents and other
authority figures no end. it wasnt that i would
openly rebel. no. the thing that drove them crazy
was my attitude which i couldnt hide to save my
ass. it was in my eyes and in the way my mouth
set and the way i sat in a chair or stood up or
whatever whenever the okey-doke was being run
down on me by some authority figure. insolent is
what they called me. insubordinate. if we could just
do something about that attitude they said. and
they tried. i got sent to a negro catholic grammar
school cuz nuns got this heavy worldwide rep-
utation for whipping troublesome colonials into
shape. during summers i got sent to visit various
stern aunts. i also got a lot of beatings.

fortunately i found ennobling extracurricular ac-
tivities. i cant remember now exactly when i dis-
covered the pleasure of reading but i do know it
was early. i was one of those kids who was always
begging the librarian to let me check out 7books
instead of the usual 3 and who stayed awake after
hours reading with the lamp under the covers.

music was another important refuge. i wanted to
play piano and sing but the music teacher kept giv-
ing me the wrong kind of music to learn. my idols
were those who sang and played in the churches
and living rooms i knew and on the radio and
victrola. i was hearing gospel blues pop ballads
rhythm&blues and tin pan alley ditties in my head
but my fingers were being forced in another direc-
tion so my formal music training didnt go too far
though i continued developing my ears.

and i do remember when i discovered the pleas-
ures of listening to jazz. my brother who is 10yrs
older than me and my only sibling turned me on
to jazz when he came home from the korean war.
he was born to mama during her first marriage
when she was still in the south and when she came
north she left him with her parents. by the time
she and my father separated her parents were too
old to care for him any longer and he came to live
with us in the projects. another authority figure
is the way i sized him up. i was kinda glad when
he quit school and joined the army to go to korea

cuz it meant i could have my own room. i was in the 6th or 7th grade when he came home from korea and liked to drove mama crazy because he wore these dark glasses all the time and had this elaborately carved custommade in japan poolstick that he carried all the time and he wouldnt work. and he liked to drove me crazy cuz i had to give up my room and cuz he appropriated the record player i had just persuaded my daddy to buy for me and pushed my little rhythm&blues 45s outta the way and started playing this jazz music on my record player. bird miles sarah dizzy billie brownie max monk. also known as bebop.

well after i got over being drugged about losing control over my record player i started listening to this jazz music and liking it. it fit in with my ideas about the world beyond my present horizon. most days i was convinced there was another world beyond the narrow and confining one i was toiling in and that somehow i could figure out how to get to it.

this jazz music was part of that other world. the people who created it and the people who listened to it were others too. like me. i guess i was attracted by the outlaw/rebel tradition associated with the music and also by the balm of finally finding people who said the same things i was thinking or who were already doing what i was only dreaming of doing. they had found another way of dealing that wasnt necessarily confined to neatly pressed hair and white gloves or creased suits and crisp ties. the terrible twin dangers of dope and illegitimate babies were waved aloft by good negroes as drawbacks to following the jazz route but advantages like having a connection to something beyond you that is bigger than you and that is at least part of who you want to become far outweighed the dangers.

and for a black girl of 13 or 14 in the projects who is beginning to smell the fact that theres more to life than shes being told jazz is sure a helluva lifeline to have extended to you to help you pull yourself through a lot of crocodile infested murky waters and what not. by following the music i met people like me and got closer to my real ungood negro lady self.

then in 1956 at the dawn of my tumultuous terrible teens when i was 14 and going into my freshgirl year of high school mama gave up her factory job and the house in the projects and went back to work for the same white folks she and daddy were working for when i was born. only now the white folks were retired and they wintered in florida and summered in my hometown in new jersey which meant that me and mama now lived up over 2 different garages instead of in our rowhouse in the projects. i was more familar with the new jersey quarters though cuz the rest of the year i was

languishing behind the high stone walls of a negro
catholic allgirls boarding school in baltimore. and
when after 2½yrs of hard labor i managed to get
put out of there lo and behold 4days later i found
myself at a negro protestant coed boarding school
in north carolina which i got put out of after a cou-
ple months thus getting put out of 2schools in less
than 1semester though the protestant school took
me back in the fall. and i survived being forced to
be a debutante who couldnt waltz and being for-
bidden to participate in the budding civil rights
movement and was able to graduate with my class
in 1960.

just in time too. i was only able to stand college
for 1year. my spirit couldnt take no more.

by the time i got grown enough to leave home a
couple months after high school at age 18 and then
move from my hometown to the lower eastside in
new york city a couple years after that and by the
time my parents figured out where i was and what
i was doing i started hearing this line from them
more and more: girl you know you wasnt raised
like that!

    i wouldnt go to church

    living in sin

    wouldnt straighten my hair

getting annulled too soon after marrying an up-andcoming success story and not having even one baby

living in sin again

taking the militants side against the moderates

associating with these projects people single mothers intellectuals fools day laborers artists numbers runners whores political activists welfare recipients and visionaries

my parents liked the fact that i was working as an assistant magazine editor but why did i have to work for confessions magazines? they liked it better when i moved to the high price spread ladies magazines though they had a hard time believing that the white folks would let me come on madison avenue wearing african clothes and with my hair standing nappy all over my head. so i didnt bother telling them about the work i was doing with the militant black publications in the evenings and on weekends.

which is the way i was dividing my worktime when my mama died without me and her ever being able to see eye to eye on the things that really matter.

the last time we were together was when she paid me one of her unannounced visits bringing along her sisterinlaw. they spent a good portion of the

evening trying to take me to task for encouraging
the children of the man with whom i was living
in sin to visit us. by this time i was tired of explain-
ing and discussing and i was secure enough to pre-
pare and serve them an elegant and tasty meal and
to politely and calmly tell them that if they didnt
like the peaches to leave the tree alone please and
to watch them walk out of my door in defeat and
not feel guilty then or later.

just before my daddy died some years later when
i was in my mid 30s he had verrry reluctantly be-
gun to accept who i had grown up to be. the last
time i saw him alive he had been moved from the
hospital to the nursing home which i already knew
meant it was only a matter of hours or days. the
female proprietor of the home didnt want to wait
for his insurance papers to be processed and was
trying to stick up the family to pay this enormous
cash deposit. or else. frankly i was ready to call her
bluff. then i figured i had better ask daddy what
he thought before i made a move on his behalf. i
expected him to tell me to pay the money even
though the woman was wrong. so i was really sur-
prised when he very coherently said: dont pay
them no money or no mind. and if they keep giv-
ing you trouble light em up! and he raised up in
the bed and repeated to me: light em up!

those words did a lot to free me from any linger-
ing guilt about not living up to other peoples dan-

gerously limiting expectations of me. cuz by now i had grown up enough to know that i was part of a whole lineage of people who have attitudes and who are insubordinate and rebellious and who aint gonna go along with the program.

and so now in the late 1980s here i am in my mid 40s reflecting on where i have been so i can better determine how to get where i still have to go. today finds me sitting on this harlem parkbench letting the early summer sun shine down on me while i flirt a little bit with the guys on a nearby construction site and at the same time complete the work necessary to bring this book to a close.

here i am:

> a cigarette smoking meat eating black woman who listens to jazz reads and talks on the phone who walks in the park dreams and writes and hangs out and sleeps late for fear of being swallowed alive by tv

> a female wage slave who has had a lifetime of mostly thankless jobs and who wants out of the ratrace while she still has enough creativity left to breathe life into the projects she has been dreaming

> a woman who has lived her whole life under the threat of bombs—first atomic and now nuclear—and simultaneously under the threat of econom-

ic racial sexual and environmental extermination living now in a black and latin neighborhood threatened by gentrification drugs muggings rape stale food and decaying housing stock determined to keep constant with the knowledge that we can create a better way

a single woman who wants to stay that way while having various kinds of relationships with various kinds of men

a woman who highly values her friendships and struggles with women

a woman who likes to snap her fingers shake her hips and laugh out loud

here i am:

not too sure where my next penny is coming from completing my first book while setting on my second and dreaming of more to come.

hattie gossett/new york city/summer 1988

SECTION #1

JUST A HIT OR 2/SKETCHES & POLAROIDS FROM EVERYDAY

WON'T YOU STOP AND TAKE A LITTLE TIME OUT WITH ME?
JUST TAKE 5.
JUST TAKE 5.
STOP YOUR BUSY DAY AND TAKE THE TIME OUT TO SEE.

CARMEN MCRAE

I'M A TRAVELLIN WOMAN
I GOT A TRAVELLIN MIND.
I'M GONNA BUY ME A TICKET
AND EASE ON DOWN THE LINE.

CLARA SMITH

THEY SAY TO KEEP ON SMILIN
WHEN TROUBLE COMES IN TWOS
RICH FOLK SAY TO KEEP ON SMILIN
BUT POOR FOLKS PAY THE DUES.

ABBEY LINCOLN AMINATA MOSAKA

dear landlord
dear landlord
dear landlord

it is raining in my apartment! yes. thats right. raining.

the water is falling freely in the living room, in the hallway, and in the bathroom.

i have had many promises from you and the super that the holes in my ceilings would be fixed. but somehow the promises have not been kept, and so now it is raining in my apartment. (perhaps its your empty promises and not raindrops that are falling?)

i would like to pay my rent. especially since i owe so much. i have even purchased money orders and made them out to your corporation. but to tell you the honest truth, there is something inside me that just wont let me mail these money orders to you as long as it continues raining in my apartment.

so i am sending you these xerox copies of the money orders instead. (see enclosed documents marked exhibit a, exhibit b, etc.) as soon as the holes have been repaired and it stops raining in my apartment, i will be more than happy to mail the original money orders to you.

as ever,

tenant 777#6k

labor relations #1
labor relations #1
labor relations #1

maid to madame

dear joyce:

after todays events i have concluded that our labor relations have reached an impasse. today you left me twice as much work as i normally do. you did not, however, leave any additional money. consequently, i have done a normal days work and left the rest. no money—no work. you savvy?

in case you didnt know, labor relations have progressed beyond the point where an employee—even a maid—has to accept verbal abuse, a doubled workload and unreasonable suspicions about the use of the telephone. slavery is over. you have to treat us with respect now—not only in a social context, but in a work context as well.

hattie

madame to maid

Dear Ms. Gossett:

I find your resignation not only immature but grossly inaccurate. I made the mistake of assuming that you are a reasonably intelligent woman. Alas I was sorely incorrect.

When you contract at the beginning of a job to work seven hours and work only four or five; when you decide on your own the refrigerator and tea kettle are not part of the kitchen this is absolute nonsense and indicates a complete lacking of common sense. The fact is you undertook to do a job which you did not do. I regard your actions as taking money under false pretenses which indicates to me a serious flaw in your character. With your attitude on "labor relations" you will never hold a job, and the only person you have hurt is yourself.

On the matter of slavery, just because you are black does not make you an expert. You are quite removed from reality and seem to be influenced more by movies and television.

Mrs. J.R. Stake

the subway poems
the subway poems
the subway poems

monday morning pep pill

lots of action in the bergen street subway station this morning
energy level is way up
highschoolkids going on a trip
playing ball with a neonredorange bellpepper that is
zipzipzipping the length of the platform
carrying on their staccato conversations all the time

*mira theres the double-g   naw we aint takin that   looka louie
rappin to annamaria   ahaaahaaahaaa   we takin the f right?
aw man his shit aint together   didya see that movie?   lucy
tol me they gon be boogyin down her way saturday   is this
the train?   hi mis johnson   you got money for lunch?   whos
that?   her hair didya see it she dyed it red   she lives in my
bldg   no dummy i done tol you its the double-a!*

grown folks going to work frown evil and aloof disdainful
cant the teacher do *something with these people?* written all over
    their faces
they mad
too uptight to be loud
in public or in private
they done forgot how good it feels
and they dont want no one else to know or remember
but the kids dont even pay them no mind
cuz the neonredorange bellpepper and their voices still are
zipzipping the platform
and the station is jumping
the bluemonday blues are swinging way uptempo this a.m.

between stops #2

the crowd rushes into the subway car frantic and scrambling for
    seats

squeezing and pushing

theres one small space left between 2 kinda large white guys

just as the doors get ready to close a white person of indeterminate
    sex flies into the car in this impossible to describe wild outfit
    and pops onto the seat

now the seat is really too small even for this persons slim behind
    so the person who is very tall and skinny is sorta perching on
    the edge of the seat and not sitting comfortably back

and the guys on either side of the person are clearly annoyed jerk-
    ing their bodies away even though theres no place to go

the person is oblivious to all this is and is digging busily through
    shopping bags and knapsacks for a book and tablet and pen
    and some fruit and ends up balancing all this stuff on his/her
    lap

then the person (who doesnt appear to be a bag person) starts read-
    ing the book very very intently and making loud slurping
    sounds while eating the fruit and moving and twisting around
    even more

and the 2 guys on either side of the person are getting more and
    more annoyed as the person starts animatedly copying things
    out of the book into the tablet and sighing and smacking pages
    back and forth real fast and crossing out and sighing and start-
    ing over

well the guy on the right of the person is about to die with ag-
gravation

he is swelling up with rage and looking agonizedly around the car
at the other people and then looking at the person perched next
to him and rolling his eyes and looking martyred as if to say:
have you ever? why me god?

and the other people in the car are mostly looking away not want-
ing to get involved but kind of grinning undercover at the same
time

and so this guy is getting more and more pissed and starts jerking
himself away from the person with the book and the sighs and
the fruit and the tablet and the bags and the wild outfit

finally the guy cant stand it any more and he screws up his face
real mean and blows off: what the hell ya think this is huh?
ya punk! or whatever ya are whadayathink?

the person seems to be too absorbed by his/her own business to
respond

everyone in the car is waiting

then just when it seems like the person isnt going to say anything
he/she speaks in a bland voice: oh is something wrong?

the man jumps up angrily from the seat and stands by the door
shoulders heaving and hands clenching and a look on his face
that pleads: hold me back! i am trying to be tolerant but how
much can a man stand! hold me back!

everyone including the person ignores him

the man storms out of the train at the next stop

old woman

you people look the other way too much
you act like you dont see
you know you see them slippin under that turnstile
lookin the other way
well god sees
yes he sees
and he keeps the record
and one day
yes one day
soon too
he will show you the record
and you will be sorry
actin like you dont see
well not me
i am a witness for my god
i see!
i see you!
i see!

introducing the next

mira
nuyorican youngblood
scrunched into the cornerseat
he only has eyes for his goddess
the olivegreen pseudoleathercased trombone
resting assdown on his knee
body hugged tightly to his chest mouthpiece sucked between
his lips
he dont need no mere lover
or nothing else we ordinary mortals crave
cuz he got his goddess you dig
but some cats who know have cautioned
a life of nuthin but music will drive you crazy man
not cuz the music is dangerous you understand
but cuz its so strong it needs all the other parts of life to
balance with
else it eats you all up
and leaves you broken and beat
or just leaves you
period

large brown man

large brown man on #1 uptown train
jacket hood pulled way down over dark glasses
talking real loud:
waiting 6000yrs for this
you wont be employed or unemployed
you will be in a cage
you will be part of my personal collection
you will be my slaves
this is all i desire
not pussies or dicks orgies cars or clothes
and i cant be bought out
i got no nationality so you cant give me a name

immigrant travelin light

braidtrimmed olivedrab herringbone stingybrim
squatting over whiteshirt & tie
under dungaree jacket
under overalls (zootsuit chains swinging safetypinned from bib)
rolled kneehigh
under black spy trenchcoat
over black kneetop cowboyboots (between which rests leather duf-
    flebag)
with myriad finegold strokes outlining
fat fluffy flowers
laden with multicolored sparklestone dewdrops
all loosely assembled
very loosely
on a 300lb 6ft6in frame
complete with olympic poolsized belly
topped by sleepyeyed
middleaged babyfat face
circa 2a.m.
uptown a-train

between stops #1

there she is a colored woman getting on the subway on her way
to work

nice day

late sunny spring

the colored woman is feeling pretty decent despite the usual as-
sortment of potential aggravations that always seem to be
hovering and swooping

she is going over the handwritten draft of her sisters term project
which she will start typing during her lunch hour and she is
making notes with her trusty bright orange felt tip so she wont
overlook anything cuz this is the last project her sister has to
do in nite school before she gets her masters degree and can
move on through to the relative freedom of selfemployment

the colored woman steps into the uncrowded car holding her orange
pen and her sisters project which is written on lined yellow
paper and before her butt hits the seat he blasts:

good morning miss individual!

this delivered in a belligerent loud sneering manner that indicates
he has already smelled her strength and panicked and judged
her as some evil bitch bent on bustin his balls who thinks shes
so hip that she probably wouldnt speak to him even if he was
reasonably cool

which he definitely aint

just as her butt hits the seat he continues: yeah she thinks shes
too good to speak she thinks blah blah blah

holding forth for his audience of teenage boy stud hopefuls in the clubcar which is the last car on the subway and which seems to be understood by everybody to be the teenage stud hopefuls area to play all of their giant ghettobox radio/tapedecks tuned to the same station at full volume and smoke many cigarettes and reefers and drink malt liquor and sneaky pete and prance up and down the aisles and yell and curse a lot without anybody saying anything

he is a 50ish looking colored man cleanly and casually dressed and well fed with a cap cocked ace deuce who looks like he aint never worked too long or too hard in this life cuz he could always find some colored woman to take care of him

not a pimp exactly

but a pimp right on

the kind with a halfassed militant sounding rap which when you really listen to it you can tell he aint concerned about nobody but him and that he is coming out of what the colored woman on her way to work calls: the whiteman got his foot on my neck and there aint nothing i can do about it but cry bag

and this little colored boy that could be his grandson is with him and here the colored man is in the clubcar with his reefer and his little radio trying to act out in front of the hopefuls and prove what a bad muthafucka he still is with the bitches

not this morning he aint the colored woman decides

not with this colored womans daughter he wont

so she doesnt say anything but continues her work

and he continues his rap

she has heard it 100million times cuz its the standard rap about how the colored woman is whats wrong with the colored race yeah thats it wont even speak always thinking you after her vagina or her money or something yeah now a white woman will speak and be polite and smile but beulah no not her she would rather choke than say good morning yeah thats why i cant stand these uppity bitches who think they too good blah blah blah and what not all the way to the next station 39 express blocks away

then when he pauses to get his breath and see what effect his speech has wrought the colored woman politely asks him if he has a devoted white wife who keeps his clothes so nice and fries his porkchops and works and pays the bills and takes such good care of the little boy since he obviously dont dig black women and the hopefuls fall out laughing and the colored man gets mad

you cant talk to me like that he roars why i will kick yo ass bitch!

why dont you shut up the colored woman says quietly cuz aint nobody payin you a bit a mind

you cant talk to me like that i aint no radio that you can tell me when to turn on and off thats what i say about these . . .

but by that time the colored woman on her way to work is back into her sisters project and she doesnt hear anything else he says cuz the part of her brain that isnt concentrating on the project is thinking on how as soon as shes finished this typing for her sister she is gonna get back to work on her film and how she aint got no time for no horse tears cuz when this film is finished then shes gonna start on the next one and by then shes at her stop.

back at ya!

1.

100yrs ago jim crow
(one of the names racism was goin by then)
used to keep black folks from ridin public transportation
one of jims streetcar conductors dislocated sojourner truths shoul-
    der one time
cuz she was bad enuff to insist on ridin
ol jim was so tuff with his stuff
till half the time he wouldnt even stop the streetcars for us
when we waved em down
and when he did
and if you managed to git on and sit down
(cuz lotsa times jims employees would kick and beat you off the
    streetcar)
so if you actually got to sit down
then you usually had to hear a whole lotta crackernoise:
git dat niggah offa dis car!
there oughta be a niggahcar so we whitefolks can ride in peace!
sojourner tol em once that they should git off
and git a taxi
cuz streetcars are for niggahs and other poor folks
and sojourner and lotsa other sisters
had to go thru a buncha outrageous changes
gittin beatup   insulted   writin
indignant letters   suin companies   gittin
drivers fired
settin up buggy pools
walkin everywhere

rather than havin to sit in the back of the streetcar or bus
or stand up cuz you couldnt sit upfront in the white section
and it wasnt till 1955
as recent as that
when miz rosa parks refused to give up her seat to a cracker
and sparked the busboycott that
started martin luther king jr. on his career
it wasnt till a few years after that
that most all of us could ride in some kinda peace

2.

nowadays its mostly brothers drivin buses and subways (a few sis-
     ters) and mostly sisters and brothers sellin tokens
the white ethnics have moved on up the ladder and pretty much
     left these jobs to us
but for some reason its pretty seldom that our bus and subway sis-
     ters and brothers take any notice of us
or we of them for that matter
seems like they be havin a pretty heavy attitude with us most of
     the time
and we dont expect no better so we act the same way
meanwhile jims modern day boys is gittin over on both of us
and now with this subway and bus strike their attitude is even
     heavier
i mean
i want them to git some more money
cuz i know aint none of us gittin a livin wage to say nothin of de-
     cent and safe working conditions
but aint there some way for them to git their point across to jims
     boys without causin the rest of us so much chaos and confu-
     sion and taxi fare and sore backs and tired legs and strained
     nerves and missed days from school and work
that aint what sojourner and miz parks went to the wall for
but how about if for the next strike
instead of not lettin folks ride at all
the drivers and token sellers let everybody ride
for free
wouldnt that be a great way to memorialize sojourner and miz parks
     & company
and at the same time
tell jims modern day boys
back at ya!

labor relations #2 & #3
labor relations #2 & #3
labor relations #2 & #3

2.

                7
nOv 1 1 197
dee R masSa LarRI
I hatez to be uh bOtheration
On Yo min   i Knowz youz
iN dE bIg Time an
Youz min goT Lotz A
stones
        to carriE Yas Jesuz
        I
Youz H   UP on dE rooF oB
dE biG Houze wiT de Madame
Living Lux   anD what noT
plez buT kin you RememBer ouR
Lil $$$$$$$ matter
                        ?
i iS still waiting - In
yO SerVan T humBly

3.

November 18, 1977
When you have finished reading this
(STOP) pick up the phone and call
Hattie (STOP) Tell her to take a cab
down to the store (you'll pay for it
naturally) (STOP) so she can pick up
the money you have been owing her for
so long (STOP) Come on (STOP) Right
now!

a night at the fantasy factory
foxes! food! fun!
dining room 4p.m. till closing/thursday disco

yeah i got the job

yeah girl i got the waitress job
it dont pay much but it is off the books so i guess between this and
    unemployment i can make it
plus the bar is only 2blocks away which means i can walk back
    and forth
and i get to eat for free so i guess its okay
except
well the boss tried to get me to wear hot pants
yeah girl can you imagine
and when i went last night to work for the first time he told me
    he didnt like my headrag
you know i was hot
who the fuck does he think he is
but i need this job so i tried to be cool
i told the dude—no not the owner—i dont deal with him—the cook
    is my boss
hes the one giving orders about hot pants and headrags
anyway i smiled real big and made my voice real low and told him
    my stuff is strong enuff to shine through the most concealing
    outfit
yeah he went for it
but what i really wanted to tell him is that he aint paying me enuff
    money to have me work and take off my clothes too
no no i didnt say that
but i sure was thinking it
then when he cracked about the headrag i told him it is made out
    of expensive imported material (you know theyre always im-
    pressed when you talk about how much something costs)
    which matches my outfit and that i only wear it when my hair
    doesnt look right same way other women wear wigs

whatd he say?
well i dont think he dug it too tuff but he just mumbled and went
    on frying chicken and broiling steaks
whatd you say
he sounds like a drag?
hmmmmmmmmmmph!
girl you aint said nothing
well this too will eventually pass
what is it like being there
well its not too bad
red and white leather
red carpeting
scrupulously clean bathrooms
none of that ruff stuff in here honey
i guess you could call it a halfassed highclass sepiatone cops and
    robbers bar
middleage middlelevel detectives dopedealers numbers bankers
    civil servants doctors lawyers gambling den and after hours
    spot proprietors show biz types athletes plus some transit work-
    ers and other blue collar types who like the bigtime spenders
    atmosphere
few independent women here
mostly women looking for husbands/sugar daddies
willing to smile and be patted
in the dining room everyone is licking their chops over lobster steak
    shrimp
at the bar theyre drinking strictly topshelf
they strut and posture round the bar—their playground—like re-
    ject paper cutouts from *gentlemens quarterly* or *playboy*
sipping johnny walker red/chivas regal they can forget they came
    from backwater georgia or deadend street new york

they can believe that they have gone over to the other side
they can believe that when cops are lining us up against the wall
    the next time they will merely have to flash their gold ameri-
    can express cards and be waved on to safety
shame they dont read or i would recommend john williams *the man*
    who cried i am or fanon on the native elite
and on top of that theyre cheappppp!
they act like they dont know nothing about leaving 15% or 20%
    of the bill as a tip for me though when they downtown in white
    places they go outta their way to leave great big tips
but in harlem they can spend 30 or 40dollars and then they act
    like they doin you a big favor when they only leave a dollar or
    2 for a tip
when i am not busy which happens more often that i would like
    i sit in the corner and read or write
or just stare into space

setting up

while the late afternoon beersippers bet on the last figure of the
    daytrack singleaction the waitress turns on the lights shakes
    out the tablecloths and wipes the placemats
she lays down the tablecloths so last nights greasespots dont show
    and uses the placemats to cover the stubborn spots that wont
    be hidden
folded napkin and fork on the left
knife and spoon on the right
waterglass mouthdown at tip of knife
on each table ketchup hot sauce steak sauce salt&pepper (make
    sure containers are full) ashtray and candle
pitchers of ice water menus blank checks pencils corkscrew winelist
    at the waitress station
by the time the figure comes out and the folks who work down-
    town start drifting in for their first drinks of the evening the
    waitress is cutting squares of butter making 2 big plastic bags
    of salad lining the breadbaskets with papernapkins filling up
    the saladdressing containers getting wineglasses from the bar
then in the bathroom applying makeup while smoking a joint
a party of 5 enters
right this way please gentlemen right this way

butter #1

only 1piece of butter a customer

okay what if someone asks for more

let me know   i will decide   dont give nobody no extra nothin lessen i tells you

sister salvation

soon as she comes in the door you hear her
and the vibe in the place changes immediately
you can feel the anticipation meter risin
everybody starts scratchin they intuition
and diggin in they pockets

> *i like that 3 today   gimme some single ac-*
> *tion   youd better bring me some money*
> *back here tonight girl   combinate 742 for*
> *me baby   heres my last 25dollars   when*
> *you gonna bring me my 9   thats all i wan-*
> *na know is my 9*

during the dayshift she does teaching mothering wifing
during the midnight shift shes writing figures on a salespad with
    a carbon for the customer
steady writin and rappin
she knows just the right laugh insult joke backhanded compliment
    to shake the coldest niggah loose from his money
and shes fast
zap! and shes done the whole bar and is on her way out the door
    to the next one
mouth aint never stopped
nor has pencil
and you never see no money changin hands

butter #2

the customer wants sour cream *and* butter on his baked

whats he gittin

fried breast

shit! hes only spendin 3dollars and he wants a million dollars worth
of extras—betcha he wants more salad dressing too

the alcoholic lifeguard

hes here almost every evening
drinking pernod and water till hes soggy
millers when funds are low
gone to seed refugee from respectable middleage/middleclass living-
    rooms his straight hair lightbrown skin and lightweight macho
    bougieness would normally serve as a passport for

teeth nearly gone
clothes wrinkled dingy toobig
scratchy greying stubble
runnedover shoes that make him walk funny

shaky hands
punkbrave smile
whiney voice
still tryin to hang in there with the fellas
just havin a lil taste ya know
when was the last time he looked in the mirror
his civil service status and his measly every2weeks check are all
    he has going for him
though these are more than sufficient in the world of the fantasy
    factory to assure him that he can meet the price of the goodies
and hes decided that the waitress is the goodies
comes with the meal dont she

and so he opens his prize waitresswinning rap with a recitation of
    the vocabulary words and the definitions of them that he
    learned in his freshman psych class 30yrs ago

cuz he heard the waitress used to teach college
then he segues right into the tales of all the broads hes plowed
and then the finale—about his wife who died 9yrs ago of cancer
the best little woman in the world sweetheart   the best
followed by the uncalledfor encore—inviting the waitress down to
      the pool for free swimming lessons
his tired old red rheumy eyes trying to gleam at the picture of her
with her big fine self
in a bathing suit
in his pool
his domain
and the waitress has to smile indulgently at him
she cant ask him how much sears&roebuck charged him for his
      lifeguard papers
she cant tell him that she wouldnt trust even a roach to his protec-
      tion in or out of the water
it wouldnt do to get mad about his grabbing hands or his stupid
      mouth
its all part of the job
right
when the other regulars see whats happening
they jokingly take to calling him the waitresses husband
and everybody laughs

dialogue

and the bitch only gave me 50dollars man   can you dig that
well man   whatd you expect
shit! i am her man
yeah but. . .
naw   hell naw!   i am her man!
look man   what she hit for
500
i know she was happy   she plays real heavy
yeah   about 20dollars a day
say man   do you give her any of that scratch
what?. . . naw
then you aint got no claim
huh
you heard me   you not givin up nothin but then when she hit there
     you are with yo hand out
aw man   you sound
squash it man   you lucky she gave you a play at all. . . if it was
     me. . . .

el padre grandioso from the hill/dealer's commercial

i had em all
you hear me   all of em
with me
yeah i was at the weddin
it was real nice
my man got him a good woman   and i had the blow
you know   just a few chips offa my personal rock for the fellas
wasnt no big thing you dig
a lotta corrections officers were there
20yr men   sergeants and lieutenants   even a captain
cuz my man is with the dept
and they were all in the room with me
13 of em
with the blow   gittin down
and then the captain showed through
and sweetheart i never seen that whiteman before in my life
i swear   but as god is my witness *he knew me!*
walked right up to me
called me by my name
asked how i was and shit
yeah everybody know me
i aint lying   ask my man here
yeah the captain took a blow
he got down baby
yeah i had em all
right in the room with me
and the blow

butter #3

we are out of oil and vinegar sir   sorry

tell that niggah to send you to the store to git some then

sorry sir   but i might get fired talkin to him like that

i will tell him my damnself then! i aint scared   what he got   a meat
   cleaver? shit!   hes a cook   i am a gangster i gotta gun! i will
   tell him!

monologue

i didnt git one fish
not one
in 6hrs out there on that water
hot as it is
been fishin in that spot for years
ever since i come up here
same spot
not a one

butter #3a

whatd you tell that customer

that we are out of oil and vinegar and that i cant tell you to send
    me to the store for any cuz i might get in trouble

hmmmmmmmmmmmph!   you did huh   well dont send nobody
    else back here

i didnt send him

you hear me! dont send nobody else back here i said

the soldier

skinny military hat
called cuntcutter
tiny neat rastalocks
youngboy face
age showing in corners
uniform of pieces of uniforms of various time periods
contemporary boyscout knapsack
deadeyes
body hunched   rigid
lips at attention for a signal
via the white walkietalkie with 3ft antennae which he is holding
atop the bar during the peak hour of saturdaynight madmagic

> *you see that dude down the bar   yeah hes*
> *talkin to his leader   naw man hes talkin to*
> *the moon   i betcha hes a fuckin undercover*
> *cop*

this last from one of the paranoid sniffers of cocaine
but the waitress went and stood next to him
and she said he wasnt talkin to nobody
and that the radio was silent too

butter #3b

the party of 4 wants extra butter

what!

yeah all of em

thats that oil and vinegar muthafucka aint it

they also want more rolls

whatwhatwhat! you charge em you hear! charge em extra and put
a stop to this shit right now!

how much

50cents goddammit   50cents! 50cents each! theyll pay goddam-
mit   theyll pay me!

1000dollar talk outta bubblelips/or: beware of he who serves

he knows you wont know who he is
so he wears his movie directors viewfinder round his neck
just like in ho-wood
other than that hes very casual in his designer jeans and plaid shirt
    and youd never
know till he opens his mouth and gives you the 1000dollar
rap punctuated by swampwater and fatback about
how hes producing/directing *the* movie thats gonna finally set the
    record straight bout
the True Beauty! (amen)
and Strength!   (amen)
and Glory! (amen)
of the Black Woman!
hallelujah and thank you jesus and the nasty ol niggah bitch whos
    playin the lead role has just
put him out of her apartment
wouldnt give him no pussy!
and its 2a.m. and hes cussin mad/drunk
but tryin to maintain his control
while he sports sister salvation and the waitress and tells them
how he had a featured part in gums the porno takeoff on jaws
and hes the niggah in the rice commercial
and an eyetalyin record company calls daily beggin to make him
    a innernashuonal supahstah
allright!   and hes drinking chivas regal smokin imported hand-
    rolled cigarettes and bustin 50dollar bills
and he still cant git no pussy!
by now the mask has slipped
and with tears in his voice he pleads
damn!   aint no justice in the world

butter #4

water is a dollar a glass sir
50cents for the first icecube
and 25cents for each additional one

the pause that refreshes

after bubblelips finally left sister salvation and the waitress were
    looking for some papers
so when the reefer lady came in with some joints already rolled
    the 3 of them made it to the bathroom
which was soon full of smoke and talk and laughter
about all the ridiculousness we have to deal with in our respective
    lines
on the dusk to dawn shift at the fantasy factory
and in that smoky bathroom it was easy to see how to nix off all
    the interference
which comes mostly from dudes who are our customers/bosses
and keep right on with our own programs
cuz we cant afford to weaken
and we cant afford to consider suicide
by the time we had finished soothing and reassuring each other
    the smoke had cleared
and it was time to go back to work

SECTION #2

UNCLE SAM THE SONG & DANCEMAN/YO DADDY

MR. BACKLASH, MR. BACKLASH
WHO DO YOU THINK I AM?
RAISE MY TAXES
FREEZE MY WAGES
AND SEND MY SON TO VIETNAM.

NINA SIMONE

THE BLUES ARE CREATED BY THE MEN FOLK
ESPECIALLY ON FRIDAY WHEN THE EAGLE FLIES
AND THEY DON'T WANT TO GIVE UP THE MONEY TO PAY THEM
    FOLKS
FOR THEM TELEVISIONS AND STEREOS AND THANGS
WHEN THEY GIT IT ON FRIDAY THEY WANT TO PUT IT IN THEIR
    POCKETS AND WALK AROUND WITH IT.
MAKES EM FEEL IMPORTANT.
AND YOU KNOW IF YOU ASK EM ABOUT IT THEY MAY TALK TO
    YOU REAL REAL REAL BAD.
LOCK YOU IN THE BASEMENT FOR A WEEK FOR EVEN REMIND-
    ING HIM THAT HE'S GOT BILLS.
BUT I GOT A LITTLE SONG THAT I ALWAYS SING CUZ IT KEEPS
    IT IN MY THINKING THAT ONE MONKEY DON'T STOP NO
    SHOW.
HE MAY SLOW IT DOWN FOR A MINUTE FOR A MINUTE
BUT NEVER EVER STOP IT.
CUZ YOU SEE
THE SHOW MUST GO ON.

ESTHER PHILLIPS

YOU'RE IN TROUBLE
CAN'T YOU SEE?
BABY YOU AIN'T FOOLING ME
WITH YOUR SMOOTH TALK.

EVELYN CHAMPAGNE KING

at the convention
uncle sam the song & danceman
(side a)

for annette

my fellow americans
and we pledge to you this evening
in the spirit of our forefathers
and mom and apple pie in the sky
this mighty nation
the american dream
from the bottom of my heart

i cannot tell a lie
with liberty and justice for all
human rights
equal rights
even free speech and free press rights
world peace is our goal
peace and freedom
remember the good old days?
let the world know who is boss!
stockpile weapons
by the sweat of our brows
restore the draft
we deplore violence and bloodshed
beat back those dirty commies
we oppose tyranny
we are the righteous and the right
we will never lie to you

now i want you to
stand up stand up for jesus
ye soldiers of the cross
and then i want you to
wipe out those pagan infidels
let the holy ghost enter your hearts
truth marches on
we speak for the little man
from sea to shining sea
and the little woman too
a chicken in every pot
and this time we wont forget the niggahs
peace and prosperity in our time
oh yessss and the spicks and redskins and slanteyes
wipe out inflation
plus the senior citizens
a brighter future
and the farmers and the factory workers
protect the environment
we is yo main man
more nukes means more jobs
balance the budget
golden opportunity
abolish public assistance
keep those prices and profits going up up up
to hell with the bottom
the american way

and in closing let me say
wave that flag
believe those commercials
keep those cards and letters coming in
give me your vote
just let me keep my foot up your ass
and down your throat
a little while longer
and i guarantee you
the next thing you know
you just may find yourself
organizing a revolution

king kong!
kingg kongg!!
kinggg konggg!!!

if king kong had been home
with his kids and his old lady and his neighbors
helping to protect their turf from the invaders
he never would have gotten hauled across the ocean
and ended up getting shot off the top of the empire state building
and what was that boy doing up there
in the dark
with that woman
anyway

king kong according to the *new york times**
is a metaphor for:
    "the Natural Child, the Last Romantic,
    the Noble Savage, the Oppressed Proletarian,
    the Black Man entering modern history in chains,
    the Third World Emissary."
hounded   harassed   hirsute
the poor boy is forced to strike out
wildly   ragefully
in a mad mammoth monkey manner
bound to bring about his own and his peoples destruction
oh the tragedy
oh the drama
oh the trauma
oh the injustice of it all

* 12/12/76 *New York Times* Magazine Section, "Kong & I" by Wallace Markfield

well
what i want to know is
what about king kongs wife and his kids
mrs kong and the little kongs
whatever happened to them after he deathwished and tripped him-
     self right out of their lives
did they have an insurance policy to fall back on
simian social security
a pension perhaps
or did kong work
did mrs kong get a job as a maid in a circus monkey act
and visit the kids at her mamas house when the show was laying
     over
did *ms* magazine or *essence* magazine do a cover story on her
did nair offer her an exclusive lifetime contract
or did she fade into obscurity
whatever
you know girlfriend aint getting no royalties offa those buttons and
     tee shirts with that other womans picture on them
or offa those books and movies that dont even mention her or the
     kids or the community

and what was this symbol of all oppressed people doing lusting af-
     ter the oppressors woman
can you get to that
cuz thats what caused the boy to get his butt beat
hows he gonna sound
a gorilla
falling madly in love with a ms anne human being who is setting
     him up for the kill

what kind of peoples representative spends his time running
    around town snatching airplanes out of the sky featherpunch-
    ing skyscrapers to dust chewing cannons picking his teeth with
    telephone poles
all as expressions of rage
cuz he cant wrap his paws around the elusive dream
conga drumming on his chest and hollering
uga booga! uga booga! uga booga!
come here honey and gimme some suga!

and what is mrs kong supposed to tell the little kongs when they
    get hip enough to start putting 2+2 together and asking ques-
    tions about this mad monster monkey
if i was mrs kong
the first thing i would do is change my name and my kids name
    from kong to something more everyday like johnson
then I would tell them that they didnt have no daddy
i would tell them that king kong was just this dude i used to mess
    with during a period of emptyheadedness
i would tell them that they are the result of roots or alternative in-
    semination
i would use king kong as an object lesson in chimpchumpness
i would call him a prime example of sitting at the lunchcounter
    during the food service workers strike
i would make charts and graphs showing how his roar was writing
    checks that his ass couldnt cash
impotent
in spite of his super dick
strong of back
and weak in mind
a willing yielder unto the slightest temptation
a pissy pants punk

cuz if king kong had been home
with his kids and his old lady and his neighbors
helping to protect their turf from the invaders
he never would have gotten hauled across the ocean
and ended up getting shot off the top of the empire state building
and the world trade center
and what was that boy doing up there
in the dark
with that woman
anyway

lunchcounter
conversation
overheard/commentary

conversation

heyman you ever see dese dudes
be havin all dese black belts
wid white stripes and shit

yeahman

dig
dude ask me say
if i do karate
i say a little bit you know
dude say he really into it
studyin wid jimgoldman

who

fuck if i know
dude say goldman got 6 black belts
4 brown
and workin on a purple/orange one

what

or some shit
i say oh yeah
dude say do i want him to show me some jimgoldman shit
so i say well i dont know
my thang aint that tuff
dude say dont worry he gonna be easy on me

hmmmmmmmmmmmph!

digdat!
well that muthafucka come down wid his jimgoldman shit
thinkin i dont know nothin
and i plays along wid him
dumb
like he show me the moves
realslow
2-3 times
then tell me to do it
and i mess up
do it assbackward
ask him show me again
i cant do it
ask him buncha questions
he all the time grinnin
bein so damn nice
and i keep messin up
and he keep showin me
same thang over and over
after while i starts to catch on
oh you mean like dis
i gits it right once
then messes up again
then gits it right a coupla times more
slowly i gits it together
then
just when the dude grin to hisself
thinkin bout the time this dumb muthafucka caught on
and ease up offa his guard
i proceeds to kick that muthafuckas naturalass

yeahman

i wears him out
wastes the muthafucka

yeahman

and all he can say is wow
wow you really somethin wow

digdat

yeah
he dont know
we be whippin dudes ass like him on the street everyday
while he be practicin wid jimmuthafuckagoldman

(slap 5)

and who the fuck is jimgoldman anyway

commentary

shaking his head a more seasoned blood at the other end of the
    counter is smiling and saying to a friend
yeah young bloods yall is bad
yall kick that whiteboys jimgoldman ass
but on the otherhand his fathers whole generation is holding
on reserve for you a package which when you eagerly impatiently
    tear
it open like you will later learn to tear
open a faggots ass and/or a bitches pussy and tremblingly lovingly
    adorn
yourselves with its contents rub
its fragrance all over your bodies slide
it down your throats sniff
it up your noses suck
it into your bellies shoot
it through you mighty m-l dicks and it will have
you so far removed from yourself and us till you might find
yourselves one nite behind some bushes with shit all over
your shineola shoes or your expensive sneakers thereby exposing
your little ghetto prince macho number as the desperate inadequate
lightweight game it truly is are
you ready

are you ready cuz in a minute when it comes
to the fights that really matter will you be
there you gonna wonder if you is as bad as you think you is when
   it comes
to resistin the draft due to a prior commitment to the peoples army
   payin
yo mamas rent and doctor bills when she gets too old to work payin
yo own rent and takin
care of yo babies are
you ready cmon
bloods what yall gonna do
now?

remember the gogo?
remember the gogo?
remember the gogo?

remember during the gogo economy/power to the people 60s those
guys who told us to make babies cook and type for the revo-
lution?

remember that statement about our position being prone the bet-
ter to make use of pussy power our secret weapon?

remember african queens soul mamas and being told not to say
muthafucka?

remember those guys?

and remember how they told us right in front of their silent white
wives that we were suffering from a massive rejection/inferiority
complex that caused us to want to copulate with GAWD! and
thereby debase their fragile manhood when we languidly lay
and loosely let the slavemaster have his way with us?

then came the cutback 70s

recession inflation

jail death silence underground on the run

meanwhile enter womentime&space

and now with the shifting of international power the bluff has been
called on those long overdue oil bills and the klan is staging
warmup sessions trying to pump up the war machines tired
muscles

say have you seen any of those guys around lately?

and now the typists cooks and mothers are defining themselves

the ex soulqueens & mamas are having womancontrolled concep-
tion

using birthcontrol

going to her place for dinner

sending out coded messages and press releases about their eco-
    nomic survival seminars magazines concerts demonstrations
    books poetry readings political discussions job actions self-
    defense classes rent strikes dances
moving on
digging out of wombs past pussies and into minds
talk about a revolution
say have you seen any of those guys around lately?
me neither

bruddah
da dreadlocks
dont belong to you

for Binah, Casselberry-DuPreé, Mujafah,
and the Washington Square Rastas

i say bruddah da dreadlocks
dont belong to you
i say bruddah da wimmins
dont belong to you
dese bold wild wimmins
you cant tell she what to do
she aint humble to no kings
like you want she to
she use she brain and live she life
like she want to do
she gonna dreadlock she hair
like she want to do
and let me tell ya bruddah
aint nothin you can do
cuz da dreadlocks
no da wimmins
dont belong to you
i say da dreadlocks
no da wimmins
dont belong to you
i say da dreadlocks no da wimmins dont belong to you
i say da dreadlocks no da wimmins dont belong to you
i say da dreadlocks no da wimmins dont belong to you

yo daddy
an 80s version
of the dozens

for carolyn j. and calvin h.

1.

yo daddy

yo daddys daddy

his daddy

his great granddaddys great great granddaddys daddy

yo daddy look like death ridin radar wings

yo daddy walk like a broke dick dog

yo daddys breath smell like chemical fallout and industrial waste
and he always up in somebodys face

yo daddy deals coke outta platinumplated minklined deluxe rolls
royce van with 16track quad deck and 3d color tv yet he got
all 13 of yall livin in a furnished room the size of a mosquitoes
tweeter cookin hamhocks on a hotplate and you got to go down-
stairs to the greasyspoon to go to the bathroom

yo daddy dips snuff wears a bowler hat and walks pintoed with a
cane

yo daddys daddys daddys daddy was the slave who stayed behind
when everyone else escaped to freedom talkin bout i aint gon-
na leave ma massa cuz he been so good to me

2.

pierre cardin daddy
eleganza daddy
robert hall daddy
robe wearin daddy
joggin suit runnin shoes daddy
surplus store daddy
skullcap earring daddy
greasy do rag daddy
pinhead beanhead footballhead beadyhead daddy
earwax toejam daddy
frogeyed redeyed crosseyed daddy
bucktooth snaggletooth gaptooth notooth daddy
highbehind bigbelly daddy
knockkneed slewfooted pigeontoed daddy
liverlip talkinshit tonguetied daddy
sugardaddy with a chippies playground the size of central park

3.

the employer who wants to pinch my ass and pay me less money than he would a man?   his daddy

the wifebeaters daddy

the rapists daddy

the childmolesters daddy

the socialworkers and judges who say lesbians aint fit mothers?   their daddies

the lowlifed protoplasm that steals old peoples welfare and socialsecurity checks outta they mailboxes and mugs they money outta they pockets?   his daddy

the groceryman who raises the prices on them rotten greens and that rancid meat on check day?   his daddy

the healthfood storeman who keeps his prices high all the time? his daddy

the insuranceman who comes round everyweek beatin poorfolks outta they nickles and dimes for some jive insurancepolicies that dont never pay off?   his daddy

the slumlords daddy

the industrial polluters?   their daddies

the committee in charge of cuttin back social services?   their daddies

the stepup nuclear power production committee?   their daddies

all the bigtime capitalist daddies

and their smalltime neocolonial overseer daddies too

4.

if you white you allright if you black git back daddy

i dont haul no coal daddy

all a blackbitch can do for me is drive me in my whiteonwhitein-
white cadillac to see a white lady daddy

i dont want nothin black but a cadillac daddy

talkin black sleepin white daddy

makin babies for the revolution he doesnt take care of daddy

the womans position in the revolution is prone daddy

speakin out about womans oppression in public but insistin on his
patriarchal privileges in private daddy

no foreplay daddy

all technique and no feelins daddy

yes i enjoy oral sex but i think cunnilingus is abhorrent and repul-
sive daddy

yeah i want some head and naw i aint gonna eat no pussy daddy

no stayin power daddy

if i give you some money and some coke can i watch you and your
girlfriend freak off daddy

do you want to tie me up and beat me daddy

can i tie you up and beat you daddy

group sex at the singles club daddy

find em feel em fuck em forget em daddy

seen at the gaybaths after talkin long and loud bout faggots this
   and faggots the other daddy

no technique daddy

no warmth sensitivity gentleness tenderness affection either daddy

60second daddy

did you come did you come did you come daddy

roll over and go to sleep daddy

5.

soldier sailor green beret daddy
executive suite daddy
maintenance man daddy
hotshot athlete daddy
porno star daddy
ebony bachelor daddy
reefer smokin guntotin asskickin gorilla revolutionary daddy
rushin off to africa where the real struggle is daddy
blissfully ignorant about whats goin on right here daddy
incense sellin daddy
loose joints king daddy
bigtime politico daddy
assembly line daddy
secretary nurse homecompanion daddy
coldbeer fishnchips place daddy
rags and old iron daddy
highclass houseniggah daddy
noclass fieldniggah daddy
passin out poorly printed religious tracts in the busstation daddy
shoppingbagman daddy
pimp pusher daddy
hoodoo voodoo poet daddy
parttime prophet and guru daddy
parttime nonskilled unemployed daddy
wont get no job daddy
wont wash no dishes daddy
wont take care of no babies daddy
how come my dinner aint ready daddy

what you mean you tired daddy
seen at the hotel notell with yo wifes best friend daddy
what you mean you goin out with the sisters daddy
seen at the hotel notell with yo best friends wife daddy
but baby i didnt mean to hurt yo feelins daddy
wont use no protection daddy
wont let yo woman use no birthcontrol daddy
beat yo woman cuz she had an abortion daddy
it aint none of my baby daddy
strip your woman naked mutilate her body kick her out in the snow
    daddy
chastity belt daddy
harlot branding daddy
drawing&quartering bonebreaking burning at the stake daddy
madonna in a crisscross on the cross daddy
polygamy daddy
clitoridectomy daddy
hysterectomy daddy
foot binding daddy
child bride daddy
chador and veil daddy
we will not have our women wearing those decadent western
    bluejeans daddy

if a woman is not a profit to me shes a pain in my ass daddy

i dont want no woman with no hair shorter than mine daddy

a woman is like a pipe you gotta break em in daddy

a menstruating or lactating woman cant touch food enter holy
    places sleep in the house or touch men daddy

women are childlike sickly neurotic helpless incapable of serious thought son they will throw lye and cocacola on you while you sleep take yo money and make a fool outta you barbeque yo clothes slash yo tires put things in yo food bleed every month blow yo mind live longer than you daddy

shes cute when shes mad daddy

little girls should wear bouncy curls play passively with pink-pastyfaced dolls and with all their hearts and soul hope to die sho nuff cross yo heart and open yo legs love their daddies daddy

yo daddy

my daddy

they all got little bitty peanut dicks

SECTION #3

SOUL LOOKS BACK IN WONDER/PRESENTING...SISTER NOBLUES

HOW I MADE IT OVER
COMING ON OVER
ALL THESE YEARS.
YOU KNOW MY SOUL LOOKS BACK IN WONDER:
HOW DID I MAKE IT OVER?

MAHALIA JACKSON

YOU NEVER GIT NOTHING BY BEIN AN ANGEL CHILD.
YOU BETTER CHANGE YO WAYS AND GIT REAL WILD.
I'M GONNA TELL YOU SOMETHING, WOULDN'T TELL YOU NO LIE.
WILD WOMEN ARE THE ONLY KIND THAT EVER GIT BY.
WILD WOMEN DON'T WORRY, THEY DON'T HAVE NO BLUES.

IDA COX

I GOT A LOT
A LOT OF WHAT I GOT.
AND WHAT I GOT IS
ALL MINE.

ETHEL SWEET MAMA STRINGBEAN WATERS

NO MORE PLEADIN.
NO MORE CRYIN.
CUZ I BELIEVE THAT I DO HOLD UP HALF THE SKY.

LINDA TILLERY

IN A SPECIAL KIND OF WOMANLY WAY.

LINDA TILLERY

21st century black warrior wimmins chant
for strengthening the nerves
& getting yourself together

for edwina, donna, joan, debbie, roberta

sisters   mothers   cousins   girlfriends
aunties   lovers   grandmothers   daughters

we honor yo bad wimmins selves

we pour libation to you

sisters   mothers   cousins   girlfriends
aunties   lovers   grandmothers   daughters

you who sing the original break(out) songs: steal away/steal away/
steal away/cuz we aint got long to stay here

you who wont bow down to no father or husband or lover or boss
or government

you who are the womanlover or the manlover

you who waylay rapists and child abusers and absentee landlords
in alleyways and on rooftops

you who resist the dopedealer and outslick the pimp

you who keep mr executives hands in their place

you who plan and carry out the work slowdown and the strike

you who outmaneuver the overseer in the fields under the hot sun
or in the factory on the airconditioned assemblyline

you who break up all madames fine china and sprinkle rust on her
imported linens

you who mix dried blood and powdered glass into mastas quiche&
    salad
you who raise children to love themselves and create solutions
you who dream and plan and work with us for the future

       with

       yo

       bad

       wimmins

       selves

         we honor you
       with yo bad wimmins selves
        we pour libation to you
       with yo bad wimmins selves
        we wear your colors
       with yo bad wimmins selves
        we eat your foods
       with yo bad wimmins selves
        we dance your dances
       with yo bad wimmins selves
        cuz you give us something
       with yo bad wimmins selves

that is carrying us through this world

with yo bad wimmins selves

we honor you

with yo bad wimmins selves

we call on you

with yo bad wimmins selves

witness us in our battles

with yo bad wimmins selves

witness us in our battles

with yo bad wimmins selves

witness us in our battles

with yo bad wimmins selves

with

yo

bad

wimmins

selves

soul looks back in wonder
the strength of the past
and the hope of the future

you can look back a longtime in these old coralblack caribbean
women

they sit in marketplaces selling fresh fish local produce imported
individual cigarettes and sticks of gum ½pints of rum&scotch
cold beer&soda brightly colored clothing meat patties sweets

they walk roads with bigbig loads on their heads arms swinging
hands gesturing to children behind them

they walk roads and beaches selling dresses and tops on hangers
slung over one arm selling small curios locally handcrafted
from indigenous foundmaterials out of the suitcases they car-
ry in the other hand

one in 500 keeps a tiny shop of some sort

they work cassava rice sugar citrus tobacco&peanut plantations
and processing plants

one in 5000 keeps a bar restaurant hotel

when they cant work anymore some of them solicit survival funds
outside airconditioned stores in suburban shopping malls

big juicy women small spare solid women their headrags ancient
strawhats silvery plaits goldteeth/noteeth bits of gold/silver at
their ears/wrists accompanying pieces of ancient and modern
clothing the whole assembled according to color and style pat-
terns neither *essence* nor *vogue* know anything about though
their coral black sisters in harlem south africa mississippi and
south america definitely get the meaning

we can look back through all of them and see where we came from
and who we are

for my sisters at the rock
seems like
we could

to most sisters
a very basic thing is talkin bout how you feel
lettin folks know where you comin from
which aint always easy
but is
in the longrun
necessary
but when you try to git them to do that
seems like the brothers hurry up and
change the conversation
or act vague like they dont understand english
or they all of a sudden is tired
or they got someplace to go to
or some special company comin in
or they gits mad and wants to fight
or they just plain refuses to talk
actin like they crazy
and you know so many sisters go for that!
be thinkin we messed up
or that we got poor taste
always pickin the last and only screwed up brothers to be dealin
      with

but then us sisters started puttin our heads together comparin notes
and one sister reminded us of the heavy rep the brothers got
the worlds heaviest rappers
right?
can rap on anything
with anybody
anytime!

but when it comes to rappin bout they feelins
the brothers clams right up
like they scared or somethin

and why do sisters go for all this okey-doke?
bein weak and passive?
followin the line of least resistance?
takin the easy way out?
                              yes daddy anythin you say daddy
long as they got some tired body to sport round
like they cant appear in public alone or with other sisters
be sayin they dont care what he do in the streets
long as he take care of home
and be knowin home is the last thing on the niggahs mind
                              home is where he goes when there aint no
                              place else to go
cuz she done gave him a license to be that way
                              anythin you say daddy
sisters be lettin brothers go with them and they best friend
sisters be lettin brothers kick they ass black they eyes abuse they
    kids
and be screamin and yellin he is killin me! he is killin me!
and yet if another sister be fool enough to try to help
the first sister turn around and try to halfkill her
instead of tryin to kill the one who is messin with her for real
but no she will swear that your only motivation for helpin is
cuz you the one the niggah been slippin round with all along
and you just tryin to make trouble
to break them up
so you can finally cop the niggah
like who would want him anyway?

why?
brothers act like that
cuz aint no real pressure on them to act no different
why?
sisters be goin for it cuz we scared not to
however you slice it all i know is that
if sisters keep sayin why? why? why?
and not doin nothin
we gonna always be sittin round sayin why? why? why?
while gettin our feelins hurt and our asses kicked
long as we keep goin for it
goin along with it
we cant blame the brothers for doin it
they got the upper hand in some ways
and waitin for them to voluntarily give it up is like
waitin for santa claus on xmas eve
even after yo mama done already tol you
she the only santa claus youll ever git a present from
and that the rentman got all the money
and you got to wait till the january white sales come
to git them maryjane shoes or that blondehaired doll
cuz change dont come by waitin
change come by movin

and it seems like we could move
seems like if all of us is puttin up with the same shit
we could sit down and put our heads together
and come up with somethin
i mean we done figured out things for everybody else
figured out how to raise white folks kids to hate us
and how to raise our kids to love white folks and hate us

how to put pancakes in a box
how to cook clean wash iron sew & mammy for 2 or more families
    at the same time
how to be sophisticated on a below poverty level budget
how to turn kinks into flowin silk that would blow in the breeze
    when he takes you for a ride in his brokedown covertible
yeah
we could figure this out too
we could

womanmansion
to my sister
mourning her mother

for brenda h.

is it really true that your mother will spend forever and ever and ever as a servant on her knees revolving around the throne of someone named god/master like the preacher said at the funeral

revolving on her knees and shouting hallelujah hallelujah hallelujah glory be to the name of this god/master person

was the preacher correct when he said that death is the only and the ultimate freedom cuz it alone allows us to go up through the skies to this dude god/master

cuz the preacher made it clear that this g/m person is a dude

and he made him sound like a white dude at that
                    although i have heard that the g/m dude
                    can be black too

i really hate to think that after working and slaving to meet the demands of various masters on earth all her life like it said in the obituary that your mother is going to have to spend eternity as a servant on her knees revolving around anybodys throne
                    riding an assemblyline merrygoround for-
                    ever and ever would make anybody tired&
                    bored&dizzy&sick&crazy

isnt heaven supposed to be a happy place

if there has to be a god can she be a committee of women dedicated to wiping out earthly oppression

a committee of the struggling women of all races classes ages and
     sexual preferences united in one mind/body

and so if your mother indeed will experience an afterlife couldnt
     it take place in womanmansion

couldnt it be that right after your mother was deposited in the earth
     the womanmansion transport committee sent a special private
     solarpowered jet for her

and the jet sped her through the horizon gently setting down at
     womanmansion airfield where a waiting steamfueled limou-
     sine whisked her to the front door of womanmansion itself and
     the committee of allwomen in one mind/body was out on the
     front porch with the drummers and dancers and poets to greet
     her and lead her to her own private suite in the welcome wing
     of the mansion where the way has been prepared for her to lay
     up and rest herself

while the music of bessie smith mahalia jackson ida cox clara ward
     big maybelle dinah washington and billie holiday and their
     choirs and orchestras flows through the speakers in her suite
     in the heavenly home your mother will get her nerves together
     have a manicure a pedicure a shampoo and oil treatment get
     her fro shaped up take a steambath a whirlpool bath a sauna
     or all 3 do some limbering up exercises get massaged in fra-
     grant warm oils whenever she feels like it

plan out her menu by the week and have her tasty healthful lov-
     ingly prepared meals served promptly at the appointed hour

get her wardrobe together

lay up in her bed of angeldown mattresses and pillows covered in
finely spun silk and cotton
sheets changed everyday

and talk on her phone as long as she feels like to whoever she wants
to without worrying about the bill or worrying about somebody
interrupting her conversation and asking her where their socks
are or if theres anymore greens in the icebox

visit her friends

have company come in

sit on the porch sippin mint ice tea or limeade watchin the evenin
sun go down

get clean and go out at night without worrying about money or be-
ing mugged

work out her deep thoughts

go for long walks on the beach or in the forest

swim in the ocean climb trees and mountains

and when she feels rested and ready

she will participate in pleasant structured meetings with small
groups of women
after theyve finished their collective chores

in their meetings they will talk about many matters

including how to make their supernatural wisdom and powers avail-
able to us their sisters daughters mothers grandmothers grand-
daughters still laboring on earth for this man

cant you just see your mother sitting down with the righteous native american women the wise african asian and latina women the indomitable afroamerican and caribbean women the cleareyed white women

the women who are the farm workers the pink collar workers the unskilled factory workers the service workers the whores the wives and mothers

cant you just see her putting her head together with theirs and them collectively fixing up for us monthly care packages of fresh vegetables books pamphlets movies videotapes dried medicinal herbs magazines and newspapers warm blankets organic birth control devices sample legislation fresh fruit juices architectural plans fresh air ideas on economy and health baby clothes military and political plans clear water soothing sleep restorative mental and spiritual energy nonnuke fuels nocholesterol fried fish and cornbread with *femme noire 2000* champagne on the side

if and when they want to they will be with men

men wont be in power of course and they will live somewhere else and take care of they ownselves

your mother will be in the position of dealing with men secure in the knowledge that she got her own womanmansion

needless to say her sexlife will be truly ecstatic cuz it will be completely on her own terms

reproduction wont be a problem since all female babies who die and all aborted female fetuses will automatically come to womanmansion plus women who really really want to have babies will make use of various and wonderful methods of impregnation not all of which will involve men

and of course the womanmansion childcare center will be the last-word in loving infant and early childhood care and training

and since they are in heaven your mother and her sisters wont have to worry about weather or laundry or budget cuts nor concern themselves with exploitative personal relationships retirement plans rent or ma bell neither will they study rape nor war nor any kind of emotional or economic ripoff and of course they wont have any problems around age or race or physical/mental condition sexual preference or class

if your mother in her earthly form worked hard loved her family and her people suffered the physical and mental repercussions of oppression and still kept on struggling and encouraging you to struggle and still kept on struggling right on down to the wire

if she went through all this

if she went through all this

doesnt she deserve something more in eternity than that pootbutt preachers paltry pronouncement of forever going nowhere in circles on her knees in front of somebodys throne

presenting...sister noblues

formerly with the original wild&free
wimmins blues & jazz desert caravan & fishfry

an unlimited engagement

bandleader

vocalist

began performing original
songs and dances at 2½ to escape
the horrors of a holdingpen for
lost children

made first recording ever
by a black person

also made first recording of black music

over 197 000 albums
62 723   78s
50 493   45s
& innumerable bootleg materials all
recorded under her own name

never collected a royalty check

revered as cult figure. first big break as featured soloist with the only the original wild&free wimmins desert caravan when they passed thru town and the wildwimmin in their brightly colored freeflowing garments riding camels   mules   and winged aquatic cinquepods were so taken with her spontaneous sidewalk performances and she with them till the wildwimmin threw dustfine burning groundglass in the holdingpen keepers eyes so all the kids could escape and so she could go on the road with them.

published volumes of original compositions. pungent practitioner of the mellow groove. lecturer. born in jumpoff georgia/reddirt mississippi/streets paved with suffering upsouth according to various official informed sources but we dont pay them no mind cuz we know the real story. featured soloists in her bands have included most of todays patriarchal tenorsax and trumpet titans who got their intro into the britelites as a result of their tenure under her tutelage.

child softshoe and handjive star

veteran traveler on the concerthall/supperclub/privatesoiree
circuits of europe and the states

composer

arranger

also known to play drums   harmonica
saxophone   berimbau   tuba   banjo
trumpet   marimba   12string guitar   piano
kora   washboard

recorded original versions of all tunes subsequently covered by assorted pretenders. they had to stop her from singing funerals and wakes cuz she would have the people falling out in coldfaints and whatnot according to reliable sources which also have it that a sizeable number (the exact figure not available for publication at this time) of mourners got so carried away till they had fatal seizures.

mae west   clara bow   and the other it girls took notes at her performances on the insides of their satinlined hems. if you get my meaning. had a fro before garvey left jamaica for harlem in 1913 which is also the year she toured asia africa latin america & the caribbean for the 23rd time. between gigs we have seen her in a variety of officially unlikely places working as herbal doctor   itinerant preacher   director of seances&bembes   vegetablefruit&eggs peddler   underground railroad conductor.

widely acknowledged by coworkers and industry bigwigs as the only one who can do it anywhere near like she do it when she really be doing it. can rock a church or a political meeting. known to go with women. veteran of the one nite stand chittlin circuit working by herself out of a coveredwagon with a pullcart for the instruments and equipment hooked to the backfender eating truckstop/takeout hardtack and drinking muddywater cuz no salads fresh vegetables or juices ever applied on the run to the next days gig 1000miles away.

upon waking up one morning and finding herself the only surviving member of the desert caravan she pawned her winged aquatic cinquepod to john ringling north and she eventually fell into a state of confusion with some people who said they had her interests at heart but who subjected her to brownpaperrolled sausagecurls vaselined face elbows & legs   frilly little dresses with 60 stiffly starched slips scratching her thighs   & white patentleather mary-janes and told her she would never git nowhere if she didnt wear seethru shimmy chemises and spikeheels or try madam cj walkers new hairfrying process and skin bleaching cream and rose morgans nutbrown pancake and facepowder and with your type of fullbreasted largehipped figure we recommend the superstrength playtex rubber tit2toe corset followed by skintite evening gowns from the fredericks of hollywood line topped off by stringy blonde wig and girl have you seen miniscule miniskirts white plastic cowboy boots and rhinestone gstrings?

when she hums a certain way watchout. craves fresh mangojuice.

most of her records and gigs were made with musicians she didnt select or approve. hemmed into using material written arranged and choreographed by others despite her possession of the archives of original wildwimmins material and her own original works. turned out tentshows and sididdy sets at symphony halls. wooed by crowned heads. used as a masturbatory image by leftover drugstore pimps. never liked being called bigmama queen princess madame girl baby. has been known to sip champagne   smoke hash sniff cocaine   drag sables cross the floor. will cuss out smack deck cut shoot hinckty niggahs and overly familiar whitefolks.

at one time she traveled in her own private bubbletop turquoise&
hotpink riverboat/tropical seagreen railway car/sunburstorange lear
jet with an entourage of 1000s including

> cooks specializing in sweetpotato pie fried chicken fish-
> stew barbeque and potato salad

> a greens cleaner & a chittlin picker

> a greenhouse crew of 84 to watch over the fruit vegeta-
> bles flowers and exotic shrubs

> lovers of both sexes

> her 39sisters and 17brothers from the holdingpen and
> their families

> her own kids and their families

> wives   husbands

> the sisters from her support group

> her 3 best friends

> people to set up the tent paste up wall images pass out
> flyers and cool out the police

> a circus that included the snake that turned out para-
> dise   cleopatras pet lions   hannibals elephants
> harriet tubmans mule   her own winged aquatic
> cinquepod which she had repurchased from john
> ringling norths pawnshop

> a 400member brass band

> a 300person chorus

> 39 opening acts

a 150member afro/brazilian/cuban percussion & dance
    ensemble

5000 wardrobe trunks and a 137member wardrobe dept

642 wigs wiglets and hairpieces   16 ½ton cases of cos-
    metics and other beauty devices   and a 94member
    beauty dept

coke&reefer depts

rootspersons

medical&psychiatric personnel

champagne cellar

bootlegger

fullyequipped spa&gym

various tv recording and movie execs

biographers publishers promoters investors legal ad-
    visors

brill bldg song pluggers and gag writers

the gang from her favorite harlem afterhours spot

anthropologists musicologists ethnicologists

assorted international politicians and financiers

movie&tv crews

a computerized communications division

a 500member plainclothes security force

onetime a buncha stewedchickenleg preachers made an unsuccess-
ful attempt to have her branded as a harlot and banned cuz she
wouldnt bring her show to their convention where they were charg-
ing people an outrageous registration fee plus more for room and
board and perform for free nor would she fuck any of them. a big-
name male rockstar secretly filmed her performances with a cam-
era hidden in his cigaretteholder so he could go home and study
and try to get his act together. do you get my meaning?

when she went broke the last time and applied for welfare every-
body thought she was kidding.

managed to get work as wetnurse   window washer   canner of
watermelon rind preserves   labor agitator   abortionist   airplane
mechanic   assassin   welder   women rights agitator   biscuit
batter beater   cigar roller   industrial sewingmachine operator
cottonpicker. has staunchly maintained true&pure wildwimmins
sound which has been an assreamer of a frustration to several
quickbuck/loosechange con artists trying to sweeten her up and
cross her over with a 101strings type of background. when the
records didnt sell they made her give back the below scale record-
ing session fees. not a single one of her 100s of movie appearances
has been worthy of her.

> *our enemies always hate to see her coming*
> *even when they dont know for sure its her.*

she has served as midwife on innumerable occasions and has helped lower the coffins of 100s of lovers friends greatgrandchildren husbands coworkers enemies into the ground. has walked the floor all nite with sick babies   closed dead peoples eyes and dressed them for the ground. has boarded in alleyways unfurnished rooms boxcars backseats flophouses&fleabags and hollow logs. they told us there was no official documentation that we also knew her as a washerwoman muletamer woolcarder glassblower scullion cookin in de whitefolks yard   instructor for guerillas in heavy-weapons   and other officially unlikely occupations but we always knew her cuz we recognized her sound and we would never blow her cover.

judged ineligible for unemployment   disability   pension   health insurance   social security   tax rebates   government subsidies earmarked for the indigent   and of course arts grants. when the special senate investigation subcommittee on how could this woman have generated billions of dollars of income for others and be broke assigned to her case held televised hearings in order to get to the bottom of this mess the frontperson for the combine of her employers/exploiters read a prepared statement in which it was alleged that her royalties were being held in a negro scholarship escrow fund although under cross examination the frontperson was unable to produce any documentation of the alleged scholarship escrow fund nor any of the alleged negroes who had benefitted from it.

judged ineligible for welfare.

escaped with her children in the middle of the night from the ogre with just the clothes on their backs. rape victim. victim of wife abuse. never collected a royalty check on any of her

albums

78s

45s

memoirs

music books

poetry collections

commercials thanks to the farsighted guidance provided by various

lawyers

public relations experts

agents

husband/managers

manager/husbands

mother of 100s now raising their greatgrandchildren. has suffered
heart trouble   highblood pressure   sugar   badback&feet   female
trouble. has had bouts with alcohol and dope. was known to suffer
severe periodic depression. almost drowned in her own tears a coup-
la times but just when it looked like she was goin down slow for
the last time she reached back inside and grabbed aholt to our spirit
and pulled on thru.

is reemerging.

has learned newtime wild wimmins songs and includes selections
from the original wildwimmins archives and her own original work
along with these in her new act. her sound is stronger than ever.
is now working out an arrangement with allwoman record compa-
ny. has her own publishing companies now for music and books.
has regained ability to interpret written and verbal fine print. han-
dles all her own business now. is not bitter or cynical. still likes to
have fun. does benefits for us when we need her to though we try
not to bother her too much. gives free music lessons to poor kids.
still accepts assignments as abortionist   heavy weapons instruc-
tor   avenger of rape and child abuse victims   antifather rights agi-
tator   theorist and organizer. has supported the careers of several
newage wildwimmin.

seeking bookings in the neighborhood at
>   community centers
>   jails
>   union halls
>   daycare centers
>   hospitals
>   childrens shelters
>   wimmins places
>   schools
>   old folks homes
>   parks
>   small theaters

known to turn it out.   even music critics have
praised her.   will definitely have you pattin yo feet
probably jumpin up&down.   kids love her.

not recommended for the
>   weakminded
>   weakhearted
>   or those with bloodpressure troubles.

is it true
what they say about
colored pussy?

hey
is it really true what they say about colored pussy?
come on now
dont be trying to act like you dont know what i am talking about
you have heard those stories about colored pussy so stop trying to
   pretend like you havent
you have heard how black and latina pussies are hot and uncon-
   trollable
i know you know the one about asian pussies and how they go from
   side to side instead of up and down
and everybody knows about squaw pussies and how once a white-
   man got him some of that he wasnt never no more good

now at first i thought that the logical answer to these stories is that
   they are just ignorant racist myths
but then i thought: what about all the weird colored stories about
   colored pussy?
cuz you know colored pussies werent always treated with the high-
   est regard we deserve in the various colored worlds prior to our
   discovery by the european talentscout/explorers

and we still aint
so now why is it that colored pussies have had to suffer so much
   oppression and bad press from so many divergent sources?
is it cuz we really are evil and nasty and queer looking and smelly
   and ugly like they say?

or
is it cuz we possess some secret strength which we take for grant-
ed but which is a terrible threat to the various forces that are
trying to suppress us?

i mean just look at what black pussies have been subjected to start-
ing with ancient feudal rape and polygamy and clitoridecto-
my and forced child marriages and continuing right on through
colonial industrial neocolonial rape and forced sterilization and
experimental surgery
and when i put all that stuff about black pussies together with the
stories i hear from the other colored pussies about what they
have had to go through i am even more convinced
we must have some secret powers!
this must be why so many people have spent so much time vilify-
ing abusing hating and fearing colored pussy

and you know that usually the ones who be doing all this vilifying
abusing hating and fearing of colored pussy are the main ones
who just cant seem to leave colored pussy alone dont you
they make all kinds of laws and restrictions to aparthedize colored
pussy and then as soon as the sun goes down guess who is seen
sneaking out back to the cabins?
and guess who cant do without colored pussy in their kitchens and
fields and factories and offices?
and then theres the people who use colored pussy as a badge of
certification to insure entry into certain circles

finally
when i think about what would happen if all the colored pussies
    went on strike
(especially if the together white pussies staged a same day sympa-
    thy strike)
look out!

> the pimps say colored pussy is an untapped
>   goldmine
> well they got it wrong
> colored pussies aint goldmines untapped
> colored pussies are yet unnamed energies whose
>   power for lighting up the world is beyond all
>   known measure

the cleaning woman/labor relations #4
the cleaning woman/labor relations #4
the cleaning woman/labor relations #4

the doctors knew.

the lab people knew.

the secretaries knew.

the volunteers knew.

the patients knew.

the clinic was moving to a new spot and would be closed for a while and everybody knew ahead of time.

everybody except the cleaning woman.

she only found out on closing day.

i dont know why no one thought to tell you before this the woman doctor said to the cleaning woman over the phone annoyance all up in her voice at being asked by the cleaning woman why they hadnt given her an earlier notice.

i dont know why no one thought to tell you. anyway i have patients now and have no time for you.

it was the cleaning womans dime so she went for broke. but i am dependent on the salary you pay me and now suddenly it wont be there she protested. wouldnt it be fair to give me some kind of severance pay?

severance pay! shrieked the woman doctor. look she snapped you havent been with us that long. only a few weeks. besides i have help at home you know and i . . .

its like this the cleaning woman interrupted not wanting to hear about the doctors help at home (at least not what the doctor was going to say) when you work for a salary you need some kind of reasonable notice when its going to be discontinued so you can pre-pare yourself. how would you like it if you were in my place?

the woman doctor then tried to offer the cleaning woman a job in the new clinic plus a job in her own new private office but neither of these jobs would start for some weeks. she never did say how she would feel being in the cleaning womans place. the cleaning woman realized she was dealing with people who really didnt care about her. as far as they were concerned she could starve for those few weeks. she wondered how long you would have to work for these people before it was long enough for them to tell you at least 2weeks ahead of time that they were closing. how long is long enough?

forget it the cleaning woman told the woman doctor. she was pissed. she didnt like knowing that she was being shafted and that there wasnt anything she could do. when do you want me to bring back your keys? because she cleaned at night or very early in the morn-ing she had keys to the clinic.

as soon as the woman doctor said anytime in a somewhat startled voice the cleaning woman hung up. she didnt slam down the phone. she put it down gently. but she didnt say goodbye or have a nice day.

damn the cleaning woman said to herself after she had hung up. here these people are supposed to be progressive and look at how they act. here they are running an alternative clinic for lesbians and gays and straights and yet they treat their help just as bad as the american medical association fools treat theirs. are they really an alternative she asked herself.

sure they treat their help bad herself answered laughingly.

the cleaning woman looked up a little surprised because she hadnt heard herself come in. now herself sat down and started eating some of the cleaning womans freshly sliced pineapple.

what do you mean girlfriend the cleaning woman asked herself.

have you forgotten that every sister aint a sister and every brother aint a brother herself began. where did you get this pineapple? its really sweet and fresh.

come on now. dont play games. tell me what you mean the cleaning woman said.

look herself said. some of these sisters and brothers aint nothing but secondhand reprints out of the bidness as usual catalogue in spite of all their tongue flapping to the contrary. and these secondhand reprints can be worse than the originals. like they have to prove that they know how to abuse people even more coldheartedly than the originals do. its getting harder and harder to tell the real alternatives from the rank rapscallions. of course everybody else on the staff knew that the gig was moving but you. in their book you aint nothing no way.

what could the cleaning woman say?

herself was right once again and the cleaning woman tried to tell herself this but that girl didnt hear anything cuz she had already tipped on out taking the last piece of the pineapple with her.

so the cleaning woman laughed for a minute. then she stopped brooding over those fools at the clinic.

she got on the phone and started lining up some more work.

later she sat down and wrote this story which she put in the envelope with the clinic keys. she wrote the woman doctors name on the front of the envelope cuz she wanted to be sure the woman doctor would be able to share the story. at the bottom of the story the cleaning woman put not to be copied or reproduced by any means without written permission from the author.

cuz one monkey sho nuff dont stop no show.

dreadlock office temp/labor relations #5
dreadlock office temp/labor relations #5
dreadlock office temp/labor relations #5

she has long dreadlocks & she wears loud colors & big earrings &
either red or orange goldflecked nail polish on her finger&toe nails.
in summer she wears hiheeled open shoes with no stockings on
her big fine hairy legs. neither does she shave under her arms. she
is too trifling to wear makeup every day. she sits in an unventilated
little backroom of a wall street corporate tower & types 100words
per minute on the word processor. in the elevator & ladies room
& cafeteria the grey flannel people with their blow drys & perms
& jerry curls stare at her. they ask her how she got her hair like
that. she tells them she stopped combing it. when they recoil aghast
she encourages them to try it too. just stop combing your hair she
tells them.

not all breasts are nourishing
and
all pussies aint sweet

for stephania byrd

the sun shines east/the sun shines west
but we know where the sun shines best
on ma-a-a-a-a-a-a-a-a-a-a-my!*

she is not of woman born. she springs forth full blown from the spare rib of big daddy. she is the adoring figment of his imagination come to life in his image and likeness except she comes with a pussy instead of a dick.

mammy.

mammy exists only to give greater honor and glory to big daddy her creator. she has no other purpose.

mammy is big daddys interpreter and enforcer. she is the overseer the prison guard the ward attendant the nurseryschool and the sundayschool teacher.

mammy is indispensable to big daddy. he cant be expected to keep up with all the mundane daytoday details cuz he has to keep his eye on the bigger picture. she is the ace in the hole that keeps his program going.

mammy provides the training that prepares us to be big daddys good little girls and boys unto all eternity. she specializes in guilt food smiles as control mechanisms. highclass mammies also use money   power   social position.

*Taken from "coon song" popularized by vaudeville performer Al Jolson

mammy breaks down daddys ideas into easy to remember formulas and slogans which she records on tapes for implantation into our minds at birth thus making our minds be her substations for daddy.

mammys breasts are sharp stones. her pussy is a bitter desert. her mind is the warehouse containing the originals of all daddys tapes which she broadcasts through her mouth on cue.

mammys favorite tape is the one that says: it is useless to try to resist daddy. there is nothing you can do. you just have to go along with the program and repeat after me the correct line.

everytime you defy her instructions and try to get a little life/rhythm going mammy will do her damndest to turn off your sound system. if that doesnt work she will destroy your drums and put you out in the street. or set your house on fire. or drop a dime on you to the f.b.i.

in her dealings with males mammy plays the passive manipulator. she worships babyboys for they are so perfectly daddylike. she gives them their first lessons in aggression   emotional frigidity competition   irresponsibility. from her they learn that their human rights include the right to give orders and be waited on hand and foot and the right to as much pussy or booty and as many wartoys as they can cajole or rip off. her boys fear being supportive and loving of other boys.

in her dealings with females mammy plays the competitive bitch. she hates babygirls for they are so undaddylike plus they remind her of her own undaddylikeness. from her girls learn submission overcompensation fear of success repression selfhate suicide. when mouthing sisterhood and womanlove mammy is at her most dangerous. the sisterhood mammy dreams of running for president on the steam she thinks she can create by raining on wimminfire. the womanlove mammy uses her lesbianism as she jockeys for an inside track to all the hottest pussies. both want as many wartoys as they can cajole or rip off.

in business for herself as an independent entrepreneur mammy never offers you an advance or sick days or overtime pay or profit sharing. she acts like she is doing you a favor by making $$$$$$s for herself with your sweat blood and creativity. she always cries broke when you ask for a raise. she also wants to own all rights in perpetuity. she will hire somebody else for your gig without even bothering to give you notice. if you ever so humbly question her ways she freaks out and calls you the last and only ungrateful soandso.

in bed mammy wants to be on top all the time and ignores her partners needs. or she just lays there and puts on a show of being pleasured when in fact she feels nothing at all. or she spends the whole time pleasuring her partner and denying her own needs in order to win a higher service rating.

mammy predates islam buddhism judaism christianity feudalism marxism and capitalism. she traces her roots back to the historical time when some fools decided to make men be hunters/warriors and to make women be gatherers/nurturers and to say that the former has greater social and financial value than the latter.

mammy comes in all colors textures languages mentalities sizes nationalities sexualities religions shapes occupations classes widths ages lengths. hair and clothing styles optional.

as long as we are willing to walk a million miles for one of mammys smiles we are in serious trouble cuz mammys smiles mean bad news and death cuz mammy is a jivebitch.

mammy is the vegetarian who wont let nobody else eat meat   the celibate who wont let nobody else be sexual   the religious zealot who wont let nobody else sleep late in peace on her holy days.

she is the heavy duty politico who tramples her lover/spouse/ friends/children/coworkers while mouthing off about revolutionary love and struggle. she is the professional victim who has blown away enough money and opportunities in one lifetime to have lasted 50 other peoples lifetimes.

she is the hinckty heifer who never speaks to anybody in the bathroom at work and is always sucking up under the supervisor. she pretends not to notice when big daddy rapes their daughters and sons and impregnates their daughters.

she is the female token on the board of directors of the international company that sells d.d.t. infested babyfood (banned from the market in most developed countries) to underdeveloped countries and who has the gall to go around giving speeches about the exciting opportunities for women in the wonderful world of corporate capitalism.

mammy has no home roots connections. therefore she is dead.

mammy is a dead jivebitch.

mammy is the dead jivebitch in all of us.

lets open up mammys warehouse and her substations and erase all her tapes.

lets trash all the pictures of her deadly smile and the taste of her putrid food and the cancer of her guilt.

lets cancel mammy from the universal memory file.

SECTION #4

SOME FINAL HITS/COMIN THROUGH THE CRACKS

JUST PICK UP YOUR PAPER
TURN ON YOUR TV.

ROBERTA FLACK

THERE'S NO SAVIOR
IN THE STRUGGLE
FOR FREEDOM TIME.

LINDA TILLERY

I KNOW WE CAN MAKE IT.
I KNOW WE CAN WORK IT OUT.
IF WE WANNA
YES WE CAN CAN.

THE POINTER SISTERS

PHARAOH'S ARMY
ALL OF THEM MEN GOT DROWNED IN THE SEA ONE DAY.
OH YES THEY DID.

ARETHA FRANKLIN

STRAIGHT AHEAD
THE ROAD IS WINDING.

ABBEY LINCOLN AMINATA MOSAKA

new york city winter poem
new york city winter poem
new york city winter poem

i wonder why it is that harlem snow lasts longer than midtown snow?

its all the same snow isnt it?

or is it?

i wonder cuz i have noticed when it snows real bad over the weekend that by monday most of the snow is still on the ground right where it fell in harlem

and if the temperature drops down real low and the snow freezes over and becomes a thick coating of glossy glassy ice the ice doesnt go away by monday either

but its different in midtown

when you shiver off the subway from harlem on your way to work in midtown on monday morning wearing all your layers of thermal underwear tights sweaters pants and your boots jackets scarves coats hats and gloves suddenly you are like the country clod at the fancy dress ball in the midst of all these people gliding about with no hats gloves or boots with their fur coats hanging open or no coats at all some of them and lots of the girls are wearing opentoed slingback hiheels and the boys are often wearing soft shiny loafers

and theres hardly any snow or ice on the ground except for a few isolated patches piled along the gutters and curbs so neatly as to appear more like a plastic visual effect which can be ordered from a supply house listed in the yellow pages under visuals comma winter wonderland

and by wednesday in midtown its hard to remember that there was a big snow storm that previous weekend cuz the visible evidence is all gone

why do you think it is that harlem snow lasts longer than midtown snow?

is it all the same snow?

does harlem get a more durable variety of snow thats been carefully bred in special test tubes and guaranteed to last all winter long or double your money back?

it couldnt be that the city govt places more importance on keeping the midtown streets clear than it does on keeping harlems streets clear?

oh no!

it couldnt be that midtown merchants associations exert pressures on city govt in the form of more than generous campaign contributions so their areas are kept clean?

of course not!

it couldnt be that the merchants and the city govt are telling those of us that live in the harlems of the city that they dont care if our neighborhoods stay snowed under and iced over all winter we still better get to work on time?

no no no its nothing like that you are always looking at the negative side of things!

see what it is is that harlem sidewalks have a built in freezing system that automatically switches on at the first sign of a snowflake and this sidewalk freezing system is connected to the freezing system hidden in the walls of most harlem bldgs and both freezing systems are programmed to do away with all heat and hot water once the temperature outside falls below 40degrees fahrenheit

and so when old people and babies and young adults freeze to death in their beds in the various harlems its not because their landlords are failing to provide heat while continuing to collect rents thereby being liable for prosecution for fraud and for murder by criminal neglect

now there you go again of course not!

see it has a lot to do with those theories about not coddling us poor and/or colored folks

about not coddling us and not making things too easy for us so that we wont be denied the joys of pulling ourselves up by our bootstraps

see if we had clear sidewalks and streets and heat and hot water during winter we might get carried away and start thinking we somebody and then next thing you know we would want solar powered airconditioning in the summer and an end to patriarchy and capitalism and racism and we would have a 3day workweek and guaranteed lifetime income and respect for the earth and an end to wars and we would have technology motivated by human need and not greed and we would have free education and healthcare and enough sumptuous food and fabulous housing for everybody and individual nonoppressive differences would be respected and nobody would be any better than anybody else and then bootstraps could go back to being just bootstraps

and then i could write more stuff about the sun and trees and peace
and birds and enduring and fruitful relationships and the ocean
and flowers instead of nearly always writing about things like
the differences between harlem snow and midtown snow and
people freezing to death while other people are gliding about
in open fur coats and slingback hiheels and soft shiny loafers

kids
throwing
stones

1.

the south african kids said: *Let us defend ourselves.*
on september 15th and 16th in 1976 the capetown contingent dis-
   tributed a leaflet which read: *The time has come now for the*
   formation of small and independent groups, three or four
   members to a group, completely trustworthy, ready for the
   sacrifices demanded by the struggle, bold and courageous
   enough to carry out the tasks of the day. Select your targets
   carefully, plan carefully, strike boldly.
soon afterward in capetown and soweto kids planned carefully and
   struck boldly at specially selected targets
they brought the bantu school system to a screeching halt
they bombed oil fields whose profits support their oppression
they made their parents go on strike
they made the police scared to be on the streets
and generally let the world know they werent jiving

2.

sitting in the back of the bus on the way home from work on a mug-
  gy evening my hair in 1000 teenytiny topsy plaits
savoring the rare pleasure of my own bad black woman words in
  print when the sound of rocks
crashing against the side of the bus scared the shit out of me and i
looked up and out of the window and into the faces of 3 young black
  kids who
were running next to the bus
throwing more rocks this time at the window right where i
am sitting and some of the rocks
crash against the window and i
jump up across the aisle out of the way though fortunately the
window glass didnt splatter and all the time i
am looking into their faces especially their eyes and now i
am even more scared cuz i
see confusion and fear not clarity and purpose as the bus
picks up speed and
pulls away and
leaves them
standing there
glaring and
shaking their fists and i
am scared

3.

these new york black kids
unlike the south african kids
are misdirecting their rage/fire and
shooting off in a vacuum while the real enemy
glides smoothly along just beyond the range of their vision
and i am scared
yeah
despite (because of?) their supposed american knowhow these new
        york kids still have a lot to learn about who their enemies are
and meanwhile
i have a lot to learn about watching my back

on the question of fans:
the slave quarters
are never airconditioned

when i went to cuba in 1973 going there was still a mortal sin
   against imperialism that couldnt be stamped on your u.s.a.
   passport so you had to go to mexico or canada or europe first
   where there was a cuban embassy that could issue you a visa
   and an airport that would service cubano airlines

also you usually had to be sponsored by some male dominated
   white leftist revolutionary organization and you had to go in
   a delegation composed largely of them unless you went as part
   of a delegation of male dominated black leftist revolutionaries
   who got there by hijacking an airplane

the delegation i traveled with was of the former persuasion since
   i didnt have enough nerve to be hijacking no airplane and we
   found ourselves staying in mexico city a little longer than we
   had planned due to bureaucratic circumstances far far beyond
   our control

while we were waiting we had meetings

in between trips via the *muy* clean and pleasant subway to the visa
   office the pyramids the visa office the anthropological muse-
   um and back to the visa office again we had meetings and span-
   ish classes (i learned to say *donde está el baño*) and meetings

well it was summer and even mexico city with its way way way high
   up above sea level altitude which caused me to fall right out
   in a cold faint in midsentence within hours of getting off the
   plane was warm so i was using my 5&10cents store imitation
   chinese foldup paper fan a lot during the meetings cuz of course
   the group wasnt staying in an airconditioned hotel

my fan wasnt even nothing exotic like marabou or peacock feathers or delicately wrought filigree or ivory or teakwood

well to my surprise the foldup paper fan bothered the white male leftists

i really wasnt ready

i really wasnt ready for the severe criticism i received about my dangerous bourgeoisie female tendencies vizaviz the fan (they never touched on any of the things about me that could have stood some criticism)

the white boys told me fans are symbolic of the worst aspects of privileged womanhood think they said of the french and italian baroque court ladies or the greek and roman *demimondaines* and how they all sipped wines and ate roasted meats and sugary tidbits and fanned themselves at the expense of the sweat and blood of the masses the white boys continued while sweating profusely themselves and trying in vain to shake up a little breeze with their damp limp handkerchiefs thus unwittingly giving gross evidence of their lack of understanding of the true historical conditions surrounding the development of the masses and especially the wimmin masses

think i pleaded of the wimmin slaves (unwaged and waged) laboring in unairconditioned cane cotton and tobacco fields and unairconditioned factories offices bedrooms boardrooms laundries and kitchens when they were able to snatch a moment or 2 away from baroque incorporated or ms *demi* for themselves in a corner somewhere what do you think they were doing?

fanning themselves of course

fanning themselves and each other while sipping cool water tasting morsels of food exchanging dreams thoughts plans and schemes

fanning themselves

fanning gnats ticks flies mosquitoes and wasps away

fanning up freedom struggles

fanning honey fanning

only the slaves were the wrong class and color to have their fans qualify for most museum displays

well the white male leftists didnt wanna hear about my greatgreat grandmamas and aunties and neighborhood ladies doing no fanning

talk about cultural imperialism!

time passed and eventually we got to cuba around 2oclock one morning

my strongest first impression was of cubanas easily and familiarly handling large guns at that hour as part of their regular civil guard duties

then i remember checking into the hotel nacional in havana near the ocean and taking a predawn stroll along the *malecon* looking at the waves and loving the caresses of the tropical breezes

then going to sleep and waking up and going out in a minibus on
2½weeks worth of visits to factories schools hospitals muse-
ums movies radio stations housing developments beaches and
nightclubs and meeting cubanas who were seriously struggling
against all kinds of contradictions and gasp! fanning them-
selves

cuz you know there was very little airconditioning so people sweated
and fanned a lot

and the cubanas had these bad paper fans with all kinds of color
reproductions of revolutionary people and scenarios on them

well you know i enjoyed myself in cuba dont you

i fanned right along with the cubanas and felt right at home

and everytime i saw a cubana with a fan i would ask the white male
leftists if she was a counterrevolutionary bourgeoisie female like
me

in barbados
passing a window
a flash into the corner of my eye

small spare black woman or child
3 little kids are hers her mamas her neighbors
they have gathered some coconuts in an abandoned lot marked pri-
     vate lands next to the guest house
the kids in a semicircle waiting their eyes big
lacking the cashflow to invest in such sophisticated capital equip-
     ment as machetes and straws like the operators of oceanfront
     and roadside stands the sister does not hesitate
she heaves a hugh rock high over her head and brings it down hard
once
twice
got it

dakar/samba
dakar/samba
dakar/samba

rust red rocks clay and dust

black rocks

dry heat

atlantic ocean breeze

rhythm

ancient chants and rituals

time

warm

gentle

giving

flowing

metaphysical and pragmatic

deep quiet

patient

guarded interior

soft bass voice

holding babies and bundles for women on the bus

bargaining in the marketplace

playing with children

smiling shyly and beautifully

slick guitar licks

dakar/samba
dakar/samba
dakar/samba

kher bann acc souf you knone te khou

kher you nioul

tangaye bou wow

pekhom gedjou sowou

yungou yungou

woy acc bakhou thiossane

diamono

ite

teye

laabir

walagaan

baatin acc saair

khoot seidd

bania yakamti

am biir

baat you noy te neekh

niongui fapp khale yi acc unbou djigeen yi thi otto yi

di wakhaale thi marse yi

di fo acc goune yi

di ree ree gou faffett te andacc rou

boumou khalam you neekh

yellow gold *buba* and golden brown sandals

red suede boots

yellow and white sneakers

hours and hours of evening tea talk and music

lemonade

reefer cookie

stewed fish rice cabbage onions hot peppers

little bags of peanuts

grilled fish with fresh lime

mangoes and oranges

evening walks

harmony

lilting *kora* chords

cool nights

neocolonial tensions and contrasts

have you met *le plus grand m'sieur* also known as head niggah
    in charge

mosquitoes

running sores and twisted limbs

clitoridectomy

moubou you m'bokhe ni n'galam acc thiarakou det melni ourouss

bottou dett you khonk

dalou dawkatt you m'boke te weekh

misic acc wakhtaan you andacc ataya aye wakhtooy wakhtou
   bou takossane diote

limonade

tangalou yamba

thiebbou dieunn

cornettou thiaff

dieun you niou lacck saffal cook limong

mango acc oranss

dokhontou takoussan

n'dego

boumou kora youye walagane

goudyk peekh

diakhle acc goute gui neck thi nootanque gou beess gui

avez vous vu le plus grand m'sieur connu sous le nom de toubab
   negro

matti yi

goom you kholekouyi acc tank you lafagne yi

n'diongu

widespread and severe pain

imported bottled water

people living and sleeping in the streets

cardboard and tin shanties squatting next to abstract french architecture

hollywood chewing gum

intense street hustling

cheap labor and high cost of living

the donald duck nursery school

absentee landlords and president

black on black exploitation

dry cracked earth

sparse vegetation

on the edge of the desert

on the verge of explosion

tiiss you revy te metty

boutee lou evian (diogue bitim rew)

nith niy di dounde thi m'bedami di nelow thi m'bedami

*keurou bante acc cartong takhow thiy wetou tabakhou toubab
     you diakhaso y*

chigomou holliwood

diayante bou mettibi

pay gou touti dounogou gou seer

le jardin d'enfants chez donald

borom keur acc president

kou nioul di not kou nioul

souf sou wow bey khar

niakh mou yarakh

thi thiatou diorgui

mouy diegue totje

Wolof (a Senegalese language and people) translation by C. Tall

fragment #5
fragment #5
fragment #5

1.

20 or 25yrs ago black people of my age group were 30lbs lighter and were rebelling against segregation in the u.s.a. and against colonialism in africa and other 3rd world countries

we often employed barbed wire as a visual symbol of what we were struggling against

there were nonviolent passive resistance sit-ins lay-ins teach-ins kneel-ins drive-ins be-ins

corporations corner stores churches factories swimming pools housing developments schools hotels govt offices lunch counters ballrooms were targeted for economic boycotts and folks would stop buying certain products thereby forcing companies that refused to clean up their acts out of business

there were also nonpassive violent demonstrations like bombings robberies jailbreaks undercover sabotage and straightup jungle and urban guerilla warfare

this went on for about 10 or 15yrs and produced a variety of results ranging from an end to most upfront colonialism in africa and most upfront segregation over here

there was a big increase in the number of african diplomats at the u.n. and a big increase in the number of black mayors and other elected officials over here

things were supposed to be looking good

2.

the other night i went with a friend to a pool party/college reunion of her friends most of whom are black or latin people and we were all about the same age

the gathering took place in a recently built development in an area that used to be upper working and lower professional class white but is now upper working and lower professional class latin and black

the pool area was surrounded by barbed wire

there were also armed guards

according to a woman tenant who seemed somewhat embarrassed by what she was saying this barbed wire is necessary to keep out the black and latin kids from the neighborhood who apparently dont have swimming pools at home and who dont seem to understand why they cant use this one

no respect for private property

and despite the height and ferocity of the barbed wire the kids climb up on over and use the pool anyway and so there are armed guards to keep them out

and as i listened to her talk i thought how in the caribbean the home folks are often kept off the best beaches which are reserved for tourists

and how in many african countries there are gold coast areas re-
served for the native elite who tool about in suits and ties and
girdles and wigs in all that heat and who have their chauffeurs
washing their mercedes benzes and porsches with imported
bottled water and the missionary school books with the dick
and jane stories and pictures

and back in the good ol u.s.a. in cities with black dope kings and
pimp/preachers and majority black populations and black
mayors black folks are still unemployed and on welfare and
white cops are still targetpracticing on us

3.

somewhere along the line many of my rebellious generation sold
out and now they sit 30lbs heavier on the other side of the
barbed wire with their dogs and guards mouthing colored ver-
sions of the same uneasy defenses of their tenuous position that
the white colonialist and segregationist tried to run down 20
or 25yrs ago

is this supposed to be progress?

world view
world view
world view

theres more poor than nonpoor
theres more colored than noncolored
theres more women than men

> all over the world the poor woman of color is the mainstay
> of the little daddy centered family which is the bottom-
> line of big daddys industrial civilization

> when she gets off her knees and stands up straight the whole
> thing can/will collapse

> have you noticed that even now she is flexing her shoulder
> muscles and strengthening her thigh and leg muscles?

> and her spine is learning to stretch out long her brain and
> heart are pumping new energy already you can see the
> load cracking at the center as she pushes it off her

she is holding up the whole world
what you gonna do?
you cant stop her
you gonna just stand there and watch her with your mouth open?
or are you gonna try to get down?
you cant stop her
she is holding up the whole world

Other Firebrand Books titles by Black authors include:

The Big Mama Stories by Shay Youngblood/$8.95

A Burst Of Light, Essays by Audre Lorde/$7.95

The Gilda Stories, A Novel by Jewelle Gomez/$9.95

Humid Pitch, Narrative Poetry by Cheryl Clarke/$8.95

Jonestown & Other Madness, Poetry by Pat Parker/$7.95

The Land Of Look Behind, Prose and Poetry by Michelle Cliff/$6.95

Living As A Lesbian, Poetry by Cheryl Clarke/$7.95

Movement In Black, Poetry by Pat Parker/$8.95

Sans Souci, And Other Stories by Dionne Brand/$8.95

The Threshing Floor, Short Stories by Barbara Burford/$7.95

You can buy Firebrand titles at your bookstore, or order them directly from the publisher (141 The Commons, Ithaca, New York 14850, 607-272-0000).

Please include $2.00 shipping for the first book and $.50 for each additional book.

A free catalog is available on request.